Green Is Gold

Business Talking To Business About The Environmental Revolution

Patrick Carson

Julia Moulden

HarperBusiness

A Division of HarperCollins*Publishers*

First Edition

Library of Congress Catalog Card Number: 91-070839
ISBN: 0-88730-520-2 U.S.A.

Canadian Cataloguing in Publication Data

Carson, Patrick
    Green is gold: business talking to business about the environmental revolution

Includes index.
ISBN 0-00-215839-6 Canada

1. Product management — Environmental aspects.
2. Consumer goods — Environmental aspects.
3. New products — Environmental aspects. 4. Industry — Environmental aspects. 5. Industry — Social aspects.
I. Moulden, Julia. II. Title.

HF5415.15.C37 1991   658.5′75   C91-093671-4

91 92 93 94 95 RRD 5 4 3 2 1

To help protect the environment *Green Is Gold* has been printed on E.B. Eddy recycled paper.

▫ Acknowledgements ▫

We gratefully acknowledge the moral and intellectual support of the many "dolphins" who made this book possible.

We are indebted to all participants, including Christine Callender, Michael Davidson, Noel Desautels, Dan Donovan, Leigh Gravenor, Larry Griffin, Mottle Goodbaum, Michael Hill, Steve Lamasz, Vivaldo Latoche, Scott Lunau, David MacLeod, Sarah Mitchell, Chris Mullen, Nick Tzaras, Robert Wauro and Fraser Wilson.

For their unflagging enthusiasm, we would like to thank researchers Judith Brooks, Peter Hall, Elizabeth Moulden and Ursula Olszewski: this book would not have been possible without your long hours and your insistence that we get the facts straight.

We gratefully acknowledge the contribution of Joe Jackman and the staff of S & A Design Group, who designed the cover.

To Stanley and Nancy Colbert, special thanks for supporting this project from its earliest stages. And to David Colbert and the HarperCollins team, our gratitude for being able to tell when encouragement or admonishment was most needed.

Finally, we wish to thank our editor, Rick Archbold, whose lucid, germane comments and directorial abilities are exceeded only by his diplomacy.

—Patrick Carson & Julia Moulden

Special thanks to my children, Sian, Niall, Saoirse and Breen, and especially to my wife Deirdre.

P.C.

To Rick, for expert midwifery on this, my first; to Stanley, for always believing I too could "bring on the bears"; and to my family and friends for supportive phone calls and care packages delivered to my nine month cloister: thank you.

J.M.

When the forms of an old culture are dying, the new culture is created by a few people who are not afraid to be insecure.

— Rudolph Bahro

⚬ CONTENTS ⚬

▫ ONE ▫

Green Realities

North American companies are spending billions of dollars to develop greener products and alter industrial processes so that they are more efficient and less polluting. This is evidence of a trend that will continue for three powerful reasons. Consumers will demand it. Governments will require it, through increasingly strict regulations. And corporations are discovering that a commitment to the environment can strengthen the bottom line.

In 1988, when few companies worldwide had made the environment a top priority, Loblaw Companies Limited started to think about launching a line of environmentally friendly products to sell in its chain of Canadian supermarkets. Canada's largest food distributor, Loblaw Companies is part of George Weston Limited, which conducts food processing, food distribution and resource operations in North America.

This book's co-author, Patrick Carson, was, at that time a

vice-president of Intersave Buying and Merchandising Services, a division of Loblaw Companies Limited. He vividly recalls the day he first got involved in the greening of the company.

"I was aware of many environmental issues, but certainly not an expert when one day that spring I received a call from Richard Currie. At this point, Richard had ten successful years' tenure as president of Loblaw Companies Limited. He mentioned that environmental issues were being reported more frequently in the media, and were continually popping up in conversations with his children. Richard forecast that these issues could become a major concern for business and concluded by asking me to try to determine their impact on Loblaws, not only as a company but as a corporate citizen.

"He was right about the problems—my research turned up an enormous body of knowledge on what was wrong with the planet: acid rain, the hole in the ozone layer, vanishing rainforests and global warming. I reflected on what business consultant Tony Robbins once said, 'Knowledge is only potential power. If goals and objectives are not determined and acted upon, then the knowledge is useless.' I began to work on a framework that I believed could form the foundation of a green corporate strategy for our company."

At this point in the story, a key player in the Weston organization entered the picture, David Nichol, president of Loblaw International Merchants. David was already well known for his innovative marketing successes. In the 1980s when Canada's food inflation was running at 16 percent, he created a wide range of quality, low-priced products under the "No Name" banner. A few years later, he developed a line of superior-quality goods known as "President's Choice." Both were well received by consumers; now the environment was on his mind.

In the fall of 1988, David called a meeting of his elite product development team. "He began," Patrick remembers, "by saying he believed there was a tremendous opportunity to create products that were less damaging to the environment. 'Environmental issues stand alone today in their powerful impact on the marketplace,' he told us. 'In Sweden, it is now virtually impossible to sell a 'whiter-than-white' chlorine-bleached disposable diaper. In England, the introduction of non-chlorine-bleached diapers quickly captured over one-third of the market, and even Pampers was forced to change to non-chlorine-bleached fluff pulp. What if customers refused to buy our products for environmental reasons? Utter pandemonium! What if our governments banned products such as disposable diapers, as they are contemplating doing in some U.S. states? An entire market could be legislated away, with the stroke of a pen. It won't be long before the environment becomes the number one issue here, and we'd better be ready for it. Our green products will dominate in their product categories, *if we act now.*'

"We now had our goal, but a major issue remained. 'Where do we find the expertise to assist in developing the line?' David asked us.

"It was a good question," Patrick continues, "and I thought I had an answer. 'Why not invite some environmental groups into the boardroom to share their knowledge with us?' David looked at me as if to say, 'Are you crazy?' But I convinced him and the others present that it was worth a try."

In the next few weeks Loblaws made preliminary contact with more than ten environmental groups from across North America and the United Kingdom, eventually deciding to work with a Toronto-based research and advocacy group, Pollution Probe, which had established a reputation for compentence and innovation. In 1988, a corporate-environmentalist working arrangement was still a novel idea, and some storms of controversy lay ahead. The company knew it was taking a risk, but it was to pay big dividends. The first corporate line of environmentally friendly products—G.R.E.E.N—was launched in June 1989. In the first month, sales surpassed projections by 50 percent, and the line revolutionized retail marketing in North America.

Since 1988, other North American companies have joined the green pioneers, but their number is still relatively small. According to *The Economist*, in the fall of 1990 no more than two hundred companies worldwide had "made environmental performance one of their top concerns." Of these, most are in the United Kingdom and Europe, though increasing numbers of North American corporations are moving rapidly to be cleanest and greenest, and taking advantage of the major economic shift that is already underway.

The Rise of a New Consumer

Let us first take a look at the new type of consumer that has caught retailers by surprise on both sides of the Atlantic. According to a recent public opinion poll, 85 percent of the industrialized world's citizens believe that the environment is the number one public issue. This powerful majority is beginning to translate its conviction into action. In the wake of the *Exxon Valdez* oil spill off the Alaskan coast in 1989, thousands of customers returned their credit cards and switched to another brand of gasoline. Today, Exxon is spending millions to improve its operations and repair its public image—in addition to the estimated US$2 billion it spent to clean up the spill.

The present-day green consumer is partly the product of an environmental movement that began in the radical sixties. In that decade, the so-called counter-culture challenged the environmental ethics of industrial society, taking their inspiration in part from books like Rachel Carson's *Silent Spring*, which detailed the ravages of industrial pollution, and the Club of Rome's *Limits to Growth*, which predicted that as finite resources began to run out, economies would stagnate. The trend continued throughout the 1970s as environmentalists confronted business and lobbied governments to act to protect the planet. Legislators responded, primarily by introducing pollution-control legislation.

With the recession of the early 1980s, however, the environment took a back seat as North America's attention turned to economic survival. Then, as the economy improved, a succession of industrial accidents and a growing collection of scientific literature about what society was doing to the natural environment drew the public's attention back to environmental issues. But the environmental movement had by now broadened its base and was no longer solely the domain of the radical. The ordinary citizen became increasingly concerned about the environment, and corporations began to recognize that money could be made in going green. Grassroots opposition to irresponsible environmental behavior began to grow.

Recent public opinion surveys show that millions of people in North America now have a stated interest in the future of the planet and are willing to change their habits to prove it. One poll conducted in 1990 found that as many as 70 percent of North Americans had rejected a product or switched brands for environmental reasons in the previous year. During a six-month period in 1989, polls in Western Europe found that the percentage of consumers who chose a product based on its environment-friendliness skyrocketed from 19 to 42 percent. As Patrick points out, these types of figures are nothing short of revolutionary. "History teaches that revolutions are brought about by less than 2 percent of the population. In North America today we know that well over 50 percent of our citizens are committed to change."

In other words, rising concern about the environment has produced a new kind of consumer, who requires a new brand of marketing. Yankelovich Clancy Shulman, a U.S. research and consulting firm, describes this new consumer as a "neotraditionalist." *The Yankelovich Monitor*, an annual survey for the Fortune 500 companies that identifies, measures and tracks consumer values and behavior, was one of the first to isolate this phenomenon in North America. Neotraditionalism, the *Monitor* reports, is a solid foundation of values, constructed from both the traditional and the new. Neotraditional consumers seek goods that are straightforward, honest and reliable, and that respond to a need for emotional fulfillment. Decima Research, one of Canada's leading pollsters, says that anyone who believes that this consumer shift is just a fad is wrong: it is part of a major shift in public behavior, akin to the public's mood about drinking and driving, or smoking. Environmental problems are not about to go away. In fact, as time goes on more and more problems will be exposed.

These new green consumers don't just look at the price of the product they are buying, but also ask, "Is there an environmental or moral issue involved?" They wonder if the tuna in the tin was caught in driftnets in the Pacific and if the cereal box was made from chlorine-bleached pulp. They want to know how much energy a product uses, how long it will last and whether it can be recycled. In North America, according to recent estimates, this group of consumers numbers between 16 and 20 million households. At the beginning of the 1990s, pollsters agree their number was growing at the rate of 20 percent per year, in spite of a downturn in the economy.

In short, changing consumer habits may be the single most important variable in the current business equation.

The Citizen Activist

Just as consumers are demanding green products, individual citizens are demanding that local communities be cleaner and greener. If you are hoping to expand, you will need a clean environmental record to do so, or community groups will probably prevent you from setting up in their area. Community action is already having a powerful impact on business. The efforts of Canadian and Australian forestry companies to establish a joint-venture pulp and paper mill in the Australian island-state of Tasmania were thwarted by grassroots opposition. Under pressure from local citizens, the Australian government quickly established tough environmental regulations, and the companies called off the deal. A similar joint-venture pulp mill under development in Western Canada in 1991 is also threatened by community action, by the same Canadians and Australians who stopped the development down under.

Sometimes grassroots activism can have international repercussions—through a product boycott, for example. In the late 1980s, there was an international consumer boycott of tuna caught in driftnets. Community opposition was the result of information about driftnet practices made available by two environmental groups, Earth Island Institute and Greenpeace. The information indicated that dolphins and other marine species were being caught along with the tuna, and their carcasses thrown back into the sea when the tuna were harvested. As a result, in early 1990, H. J. Heinz Company, North America's largest producer of canned tuna launched a line of "dolphin-safe tuna," which was purchased from fleets that used different harvesting techniques. The company's pre-emptive move was quickly imitated by its competitors.

Community activism has become so powerful because it arises from a natural human impulse for self-preservation. This impulse has been nicknamed NIMBY, an acronym for "not in my backyard." North America's growing garbage crisis is one target of such local activism: when a municipal dump fills up, it is no longer so simple for the city council to select and prepare a new site. Citizens invariably object when the site is close to their homes. The NIMBY phenomenon extends to any hazardous activity and its impact is enormous: since the 1970s, no ground has been broken in the United States for a new nuclear power plant, a major hazardous waste facility or an international airport. In many areas drug treatment centers, halfway houses and prisons have been halted. And this activism is spreading. In fact, no corporate sector is immune to NIMBY pressures. North American forestry giants are currently facing class action suits launched by environmental groups on behalf of the indigenous people who live on the land targeted for logging. The burden of proof for environmental safety now lies with the developer of any new project—a major change in direction from a decade ago.

Tougher Regulations

Concern for the environment and a willingness to do something about it is also turning the ballot box green. It is this fact as much as anything that accounts for the trend towards ever more stringent environmental regulations. Fully 15 percent of British citizens voted for the Green Party in the 1987 election, and 10 percent of the seats in the European Community parliament are now occupied by Greens. U.S. President George Bush has said he wants to be known as the first green president, and a green policy statement has become a crucial part of almost every successful North American politician's platform. Voters are saying they don't want a Green party—they want all parties to go green, and they want governments to force business to clean up its act.

One recent piece of proposed legislation—California's wide ranging Environmental Quality Act of 1990—shows just how far government regulations may soon go. "Big Green," as the initiative was called, linked a diverse set of environmental issues as a single unit. The Act's key features included measures to combat global warming and control pesticide use, to establish an oil spill clean-up fund and provide protection for California's virgin redwood forests. Big Green was defeated because of its unusual complexity, but observers expect that similarly strong single-issue legislation will be introduced and accepted.

Of immediate concern to North American companies is the appearance of green trade barriers. According to the European Community (EC), national environmental standards are one of the fastest-growing forms of non-tariff barriers within the EC, where environmental requirements are generally much stricter than here. And as Europe moves to harmonize its rules for product quality, this huge market will become increasingly difficult for North American firms to penetrate unless their own products meet or exceed European standards. This trend may well be reinforced as the cleaner countries adopt green tariffs to keep out underpriced goods from more polluting jurisdictions. Until recently, for example, Japan lagged behind the West in developing and enforcing environmental laws. Today, this country, where raw materials are at a premium, has some of the most restrictive antipollution legislation in the world.

Increasingly, environmental control and regulations will need to be viewed in an international context. Already, there is an increase in the number of agreements that transcend national borders and trading blocs to regulate global pollution. The best known of these, the Montreal Protocol, was signed in September 1987 by twenty-four Western governments. It restricted the production of ozone-depleting agents and stipulated a freezing of chlorofluorocarbons (CFCs) at 1986 levels by 1989, and a halving of production by 1998. Most signatories have either complied with or exceeded these goals, and individual companies are establishing their own standards that surpass those called for in the Protocol.

Regulations are not just a source of problems for business. Tough environmental standards also mean opportunities for the greenest companies and open up whole new markets. For example, the cost reductions realized through innovations such as waste management can end up on the bottom line, as we discuss in Chapter Four, "Clean Up Your Own Act." Regulations are also an incentive to develop alternative technologies and processes. For instance, the U.S. market for scrubbers that remove the acid in emissions from coal-fired electricity-generating stations is now worth US$2 billion annually. And chemical giants such as Du Pont and Rhone-Poulenc have opened environmental clean-up businesses. Today, the market for pollution control and clean-up represents about US$120 billion annually in North America, and is growing at 7.5 percent per annum; in Europe, the market is roughly the same size, while in the Pacific Rim, the investment equals about US$55 billion.

Geonomics and the Bottom Line

As the green business revolution accelerates, a new economic theory is gaining acceptance—"geonomics." This theory describes a system where economic growth can be combined with the preservation of the natural environment. Its exponents point out that until recently many of the hidden costs of economic growth have not been accounted for. Björn Stigson, who runs the Swedish engineering firm A.B. Fläkt: "We treat nature like we treated workers a hundred years ago. We included then no cost for the health and social security of workers in our calculations, and today we include no cost for the health and security of nature." Instead, these costs were borne by society as a whole in the form of ever-diminishing resources, the extinction of potentially valuable plants and animals, health problems, global warming, depletion of the ozone layer and so on. For example, the costs in terms of human health and environmental damage of noxious gases released into the atmosphere from a polluting factory are not now usually included on that factory's balance sheet or in the price the consumer pays for its products.

When Patrick is talking to business groups, he likes to remind his audience that it is only recently that all these hidden costs of our industrial society have become a concern because of the speed of economic growth, the population explosion and the extraordinary rise in industrial productivity. "Who could have predicted that what it took the world's economy one year to produce at the beginning of this century can now be produced in a two-week period?" he asks. "If we don't find ways to preserve our diminishing resources and to protect basic necessities of life such as the cleanliness of the air we breathe, then these hidden costs will soon put us all out of business. Geonomics is simply a recognition of the integral relationship between the economy of a country and its irreplacable natural assets."

Geonomists talk about finding the best ways to "internalize" these hidden environmental costs, ways that use the law of supply and demand, the basic mechanism of the free market. There are already a number of ways in which these costs are starting to show up on the balance sheet. The main one is the stricter government regulation we have just discussed. For example, stringent Canadian government emissions standards have caused Inco, the giant mining company, to make a massive investment in pollution-abatement equipment at its plant in Sudbury, Ontario, in effect making the price of nickel reflect to some degree the cost of keeping the air clean. The marketplace is also being increasingly pressured to take environmental costs into account in the form of liability insurance. As the consequences of poor environmental practices become more costly (huge fines, executives sent to jail, plants shut down), the cost of insurance also rises. Insurers have begun to refuse to sell policies to companies that refuse to clean up their operations. As this trend continues, the cost of doing business in every economic sector will increasingly reflect true environmental costs.

Eventually, geonomists believe, everything we do that has an environmental impact will have a dollar figure attached to it. Not only will polluting cars and trucks be prohibitively expensive (or impossible to find), but their owners will have to pay a penalty for less-than-clean exhaust. Waste disposal will become much more costly: some U.S. cities already have a user-pay system for residential garbage collection. Every company from the resource sector to the service sector will discover that there is a strong economic incentive to get more out of less, and to use everything in a cleaner way. In essence, this will mean that society will stop living off the capital, the finite resources of the planet, and begin living off what that capital can earn, just as if it were invested in an interest-bearing security. In truth, geonomics is already here, although it is not yet universal. The examples that exist today point the way toward the emerging business climate of tomorrow.

The clearest sign of society's turn toward this new economic principle was the publication, in 1987, of the report of the World Commission on Environment and Development (WCED). The Commission's report, *Our Common Future*, thrust the inextricably linked issues of environment and economy onto center stage. *The Brundtland Report*, as it is commonly called, after the Commission Chair, Norwegian Prime Minister Gro Harlem Brundtland, was revolutionary in its departure from the findings of previous environmental reports. It was targeted at two groups who had no interest in the old-school "limits to growth" theories: business and the developing world. Brundtland's group knew two things:

1. that of all activities business has the greatest impact on the environment, so its support was crucial and
2. that developing countries like China and India have no intention of depriving their citizens of the fruits of industrialization—goods such as automobiles, refrigerators and microwave ovens.

The solution had been floating around in environmental circles since the 1970s, but with the report's publication it became the rallying cry for business and government around the world. It is summed up in the phrase "sustainable development," which, according to Patrick, were the two most important words in the report.

Sustainable development was defined as "development that meets the needs of the present without compromising the ability of future generations to meet their own needs." The message was that promoting economic growth and preserving the planet are compatible. "We see ... the possibility for a new era of economic growth, one that must be based on policies that sustain and expand the environmental resource base," the report stated. The earth's growing environmental crisis was viewed positively, as an opportunity rather than a problem.

The simple phrase "sustainable development" carries an important message for industry. "You don't have to close up shop to save the planet," says Patrick. "In fact, the report told us, environmental issues must be viewed from a business perspective. Take natural resources as an example: if we are to develop them sustainably, we must manage them conservatively, continually reinvest, or risk depleting our capital. This revelation has spawned the green business revolution."

Critics argue that sustainable development is a vague notion, that it represents wishful thinking rather than an economic game plan. But sustainable development's ambiguity is also its strength; defining it further would limit its possibilities. It points the direction; the details will be filled in as we go along. "It's both simple and complex at the same time," says Pat Delbridge, a respected environmental consultant and member of Canada's National Task Force on Environment and Economy. "On the one hand you have the motherhood issue: that you can't destroy our grandchildren's future; an idea with which everyone agrees. On the other hand, how do you balance economic development and protection of the natural environment?"

Sustainable development means natural resources and other environmental assets will be managed both for the short-term benefit of society *and* with long-term interests in mind. For business, this will mean altering or eliminating practices that give rise to environmental problems. Without such a rethinking, the authors of the report realized, we will not only destroy what's left of the natural environment, but also lose our opportunity for continued economic well-being.

As the decade of the 1990s begins, green means different things to different companies. Many—perhaps the majority—are still resisting or actually fighting the radical shift in the marketplace. But the pioneers have already realized that greening must be done, and that those who don't initiate greener ways of operating will be forced to change—by demanding consumers and government regulators—or they will go out of business. "Corporations that think they can drag their heels indefinitely on environmental problems should be advised: society won't tolerate it," says Du Pont chairman E. S. Woolard, "and Du Pont and other companies with real sensitivity and environmental commitment will be there to supply your customers after you're gone."

If you have picked up this book because you want your company to successfully navigate the tricky waters of the green business revolution, you have come to the right place. *Green Is Gold* is the first practical guide for companies who want to go green. It is both a sourcebook and a how-to book. It gathers together the key information about what the green pioneers are already doing and about the specific factors that are pushing the North American economy toward green. And it gives you the best advice—from our own experience and the experience of other companies on the cutting edge—on how to make the transition with a maximum of profit and a minimum of aggravation.

The environment is the primary issue currently facing the North American economy. Green consumers, green regulations, green trade barriers and high environmental standards together represent a powerful social and economic force that no company can safely ignore. The demand for products and services that "don't cost the earth" will continue to grow. And the biggest business opportunity of the coming decade and the next century lies in your company's ability to turn green into gold.

▫ TWO ▫
Develop a Green Strategy

Now that you have decided you want to steer your company in a green direction, your first step is to develop a green strategy. This should include a statement of basic principles and an outline of the overall direction you want to take. It should also identify the specific areas you intend to concentrate on. It may not carry a time frame other than "as fast as we can," but it should answer the following questions: (1) where are we now? (2) where do we want to/have to go? (3) how do we get there?

Your green plan must be different from any strategy before it. It is not just a statement of intent, but the first expression your company makes of a collective psychological shift. It is the first sign that you will be using new criteria as you make your day-to-day business decisions. "Nothing short of a new corporate mindset is required," says Patrick. "The greening that is underway in the business community represents a fundamental shift in the way we make decisions, set objectives and operate."

The key to the development of any sound strategy, green or

otherwise, is accurate and complete information and the avoidance of premature decisions, especially when on unfamiliar ground. As part of this process, develop a monitoring network to keep you up to date on changes in the marketplace and evolving green consumer attitudes. You will require detailed knowledge of environmental issues and how they affect your business. You will need to know what issues government regulators are targeting, what your competitors are planning and what is transpiring in other countries. Before you can lay out a green strategy, you need to gather all the facts about the ways in which the green business revolution is affecting your sector and your company and then figure out what these facts mean to you. In short, you must gather the best and latest environmental intelligence and analyze it thoroughly. As your company makes its green transition, this will become an ongoing activity.

Of course, many organizations will move into the green business arena without taking the time to think through their long-term goals and specific objectives. In the real world when one of your competitors is about to introduce a new line of environmentally friendly products you may not have much time for corporate soul-searching. This is what happened at Loblaws, which developed its G.R.E.E.N line first because it saw the tremendous opportunity for these products and because it wanted to pre-empt its competitors in this important new market.

"In the research and development stage of the G.R.E.E.N line," Patrick reflects, "we asked: 'How do our products measure up in a green marketplace?' 'What changes do they require to become greener?' 'How do we make, communicate and sustain these changes?' The questions themselves and the development process made us realize how important it was to look at the big picture, and to think about where we wanted to go in the future."

In this way, the development of the products provided the impetus for the overall greening of the company. Once the initial products were on the shelf, Loblaws began to understand the far-reaching implications of what they had begun. Today, Loblaws has devised a more comprehensive set of green goals and objectives. While developing a green strategy is time-consuming, and by its very nature evolutionary, we believe strongly that it pays to think through your corporate commitment to the environment.

Green Business 101

There is no secret formula for green information-gathering. Like most research, it takes patience and hard work. In 1988, when Loblaws first decided the environment was a priority, it was astonishing how little business people knew about this enormous and complex subject. That situation is now changing, but ignorance of environmental issues is still the norm, rather than the exception. When Patrick was commissioned by Richard Currie to research environmental issues and their impact on the company, he realized he had a challenging task ahead of him. No courses were offered on business and the environment, so he embarked on a self-directed and very intensive course of study that he likes to call Green Business 101. It consisted of attending meetings and conferences, participating in discussions with environmental groups and above all reading extensively. He began by reading everything he could get his hands on, from scientific articles about global warming to pieces on organic methods of farming. "When all is said and done," he says now, "*The Brundtland Report* was the most useful book I read. It gave me the overview, the framework in which to fit the other information I was collecting." He also recommends journalist Warner Troyer's *Preserving Our World*, which provides an excellent synopsis of the Brundtland Report in just over one hundred pages. The best advice we can give is to read widely, including environmental magazines with strange names like *Buzzworm* and *Garbage*, and the green consumer guides we discuss later in this chapter. Organizations ranging from think tanks to business associations to environmental groups are publishing insightful material on the emerging business issues and chronicling sustainable development success stories. You will find a selected list of these resources in the Green Business Library at the back of this book.

One of the conferences Patrick attended was The World Conference on the Changing Atmosphere, held in Toronto in June 1988. It brought together three hundred scientists and government policy makers from forty-eight countries to discuss the effects of global warming and to investigate possible solutions. An immense amount of knowledge was gathered in one location, but on the first day of the conference businesspeople were virtually absent. Patrick recalls, "Listening to the various reports on global issues made me realize that even though global warming was not an issue of immediate concern to Loblaws, its long-term impact on business could be enormous. And the potential of the scientific data presented was also enormous. The companies that could find ways to solve these problems would reap huge benefits, yet the firms who contribute most to warming through carbon dioxide emissions were not in attendance.

"At the end of the conference's first day I telephoned some of Loblaws' major suppliers, including Coca-Cola and Atlantic Packaging, and the vice president of the Retail Council of Canada. I explained the purpose of the conference and why I believed it was important for them to attend." As a result all of the companies sent representatives. By the end of the conference, they acknowledged the seriousness of the situation and returned to their respective firms with a greater understanding of the relationship between business and one of the major environmental issues of the day. Patrick then prepared a report on the conference and distributed it within Loblaws. From the positive feedback he received, it was apparent that executives throughout the organization were very interested in finding ways to make Loblaws more environmentally friendly. This in itself was encouraging information and an excellent basis on which to build in developing a corporate response to environmental issues.

In 1988 it was equally rare to find a businessperson at a gathering of environmental groups, who were then still generally regarded as the enemy. Shortly after the Changing Atmosphere conference, Patrick attended the Earth Day Festival in Halifax, Nova Scotia, because he wanted to hear as many different points of view as possible. Just as at the Toronto conference, he was the lone business representative, but this time he was making a different kind of statement.

About twenty environmental organizations from across the province had gathered to informally discuss their concerns. It was an open-air affair, with booths set up around the perimeter of a farmer's field. Under the broiling sun, Patrick cut a distinct figure in his suit and tie. He hoped his appearance said, "I'm a businessman here to learn." But he recalls that when he first arrived the environmentalists ignored him, or stared at him as if he were from another planet. However, as the day wore on, and people began to see his concern for environmental issues was genuine, he was able to break through their collective reserve (and animosity), establishing some important connections that would later assist him greatly in coming to terms with his assigned task. "I told them quite frankly that most businesses were only beginning to wake up to the importance of the environment," he remembers, "but that things were about to change. And fast."

These anecdotes illustrate how important it is, particularly in the early stages of corporate greening, to seek information wherever you can find it. Places and sources you may have traditionally ignored or dismissed may be among the most fruitful. Later in this chapter, we will discuss some of these non-traditional sources in more detail—particularly environmental groups and environmental consultants. But there is already a burgeoning green information industry that you can tap into.

For example, many business organizations are engaged in ongoing information-gathering or major studies. As this book goes to press, Canada's Business Council on National Issues (BCNI), a coalition of the country's biggest companies, has asked its Environmental Task Force to prepare a report that will profile companies on the leading edge and include recommendations for BCNI's members. Coalitions of business groups and moderate environmentalists are busy grappling with similarly diverse issues. For example, the U.S. Corporate Conservation Council, which includes senior corporate executives and representatives of the World Wildlife Fund (WWF), is developing green business models and an environmental code of ethics. Finally, task forces and round tables are bringing business, government and environmentalists to the same table. In 1989 Canada's National Task Force on Environment and Economy brought together seven senior government ministers, the same number of senior corporate officers, two professional environmentalists and one academic to discuss the ways each sector could work to bring the concepts of sustainable development into the mainstream. Each of these organizations is releasing reports and making recommendations that businesses should note.

At the end of his initial research phase, Patrick had a reasonable grasp of the whole array of environmental problems that are currently confronting the planet: ozone depletion, global warming, waste disposal, air and water pollution, disappearing habitat and vanishing species. He had learned how fast the Amazon rainforest was being cut down, and about the indiscriminate slaughter of marine life caused by driftnet fishing in the Pacific Ocean. Less clear to him were the specific facts and issues that would have an immediate impact on his own business—food retailing—in the near term.

Figure Out How the
Key Facts Affect Your Business

The next stage in developing your corporate green strategy is to isolate the key environmental, societal and economic factors that will affect your business, then determine how to respond to these new realities. In the Loblaws case, some of these facts were fairly obvious. The company knew that European consumers were demanding greener products and predicted that North Americans would soon catch up. It knew that issues such as the environmental impact of a product and how it was packaged or overpackaged were very high on consumers' lists of concerns. However, as Patrick's research continued, he learned that there was a large number of other facts to consider.

Focus on Environmental Issues

Corporate greening is largely a result of the growing public concern about environmental issues, a concern that will only grow over the coming decade. Scientists and environmentalists warn that new and disturbing information about our ecological problems will continue to come to light and more environmental catastrophes will hit the headlines. It is therefore essential to track current and emerging enviromental issues continuously for their specific impact on your industry.

This is often more complicated than it might first appear. When Loblaws looked at the issues most directly relevant to a supermarket chain, the list seemed relatively straightforward. The shortage of landfills was of increasing concern, recycling programs were being launched in major cities throughout Canada and consumers were beginning to complain about excess packaging. The solution seemed obvious: ask suppliers to begin designing more environmentally benign containers. As it turned out, matters were much more complex than anyone imagined. When the company traced the path that packaging follows from its origins to its disposal, the complexity and interdependence of the related environmental problems became obvious. Whether paper, glass, plastic or metal, all packaging begins with the extraction or harvesting of raw materials. However, our current resource management practices are considered to be unsustainable, so how do you decide if one type of raw material is better than another in terms of its environmental impact? Choosing a paper package (made from a renewable resource) over plastic (made from nonrenewable oil) may seem preferable until you get to the end of the path, where you have to throw the package away. Then, if the paper packaging is not recyclable, will it end up in landfills where it already contributes 30 percent of the total volume? In which case a thin plastic wrapper may be preferable, since it takes up less space in a landfill. But plastic won't break down. It's not biodegradable, so maybe paper is the wise choice after all. This is only one of the many dilemmas we face.

It is crucial that your company understand the interrelatedness of environmental issues—even those that don't at first glance appear to be linked to your business—so that you can devise alternatives that don't simply create a new problem while solving an old one. Each economic sector is faced with particular issues connected to its way of operating. For example, the forestry sector is facing growing concern about its methods of harvesting and its reforestation policies, while all chemical companies are grappling with the vexing problems of toxic waste. The challenge in developing your green strategy is not only to decide which issues are of most immediate concern to you, but to see beyond these specific issues to the whole network of related concerns.

All companies can and should perform the kind of fact finding and analysis that Loblaws undertook. Your analysis should cover the impact of the environmental issues on each area of your operations, and how each immediate issue you face connects to larger green concerns. This process should help you zero in on the most pressing issues, and it will help you think your way through the maze of environmental problems, not just those that are currently receiving the most publicity. At the very least, the process will help you to see what is fundamentally at stake as North America struggles to integrate environmental and economic concerns at every level.

Keep Tabs on the Emerging Green Consumer

Discovering what the rise of the green consumer will mean to your company is central to your green business strategy. Tracking environmental issues will help you to do this because the next hot issue will soon enough translate into a new demand by green consumers. This is one of the reasons why it is important to keep an eye on jurisdictions that are more advanced than your own, such as Europe, or those that are North American pioneers, such as California and Ontario. In particular, read green consumer guides as soon as they are published, and look at regular updates as well.

These guides identify the links between purchases and their environmental impact, and give the consumer a chance to do something about it. The guides do the consumer's homework, by identifying the links between companies and suppliers, and probing corporate records on any number of environmental (and humanitarian) issues. They enable newly educated shoppers to ask questions, learn about sources of supply and methods of manufacture, choose one retailer, manufacturer or product over another, or request alternative products. The guides urge shoppers to vote with their wallets and, in doing so, push industry in a more environmentally responsible direction. Chances are that one of your products or one of its components—or your whole company—will be critiqued in a green consumer guide, if it hasn't been already. Even if your product is a small part of something consumers buy, you are not immune to the risk of being labeled environmentally insensitive.

The Green Consumer Guide, first of its kind, was published in the United Kingdom in 1987. Today, versions have been released in ten countries, with combined sales topping a million copies. A Canadian edition, released in 1989, has sold more than 175,000 copies, and a U.S. edition will be published in 1991.

According to Patrick, the guides are important for two reasons, "One, because they generate a great deal of consumer awareness about the environmental impact of purchasing decisions, and two, because they make producers rethink their products as well. It's not just consumers who are buying them, but businesspeople also. David Nichol says that when he first discovered *The Green Consumer Guide* while on a buying trip in the U.K., he thought it was 'a book only the author's parents would buy.' He was astounded to see it on the bestseller list a week later, and brought back copies for our senior management team."

Susan Hayward, vice-president of Yankelovich Clancy Shulman, notes, however, that there is one central problem with the guides: the information that is available, the solutions and the issues are changing so fast that the guides go quickly out of date. "Take biodegradability as an example," she says. "A year ago, we all thought biodegradable plastic was the way to go. Today, we know that's not true." But regardless of how current the information is, the green guides are a powerful manifestation of changing consumer demand. (In addition, consumer associations, public opinion surveys and even your own staff are excellent sources of information on greener buying practices.)

In the near future the new green consumers will have an impact on your business. Forecasting what this impact will be is part of developing a green strategy that is right for your company.

Keep Ahead of Government Regulations

As we have already discussed, one of the two main engines driving the green business revolution is government regulation. As you develop your green strategy, you need to know not only all the ramifications of the regulations currently on the books, but where government regulations are heading both in your jurisdiction and in your export markets. As a result of intense lobbying by business, some of the more punitive regulations are being modified or postponed. However, there is no doubt that laws designed to protect the environment will continue to get tougher.

It is crucial to keep track of existing legislation, to ensure that you are in compliance with it and to monitor new developments. Assign this responsibility to a top-level executive, although it could also be shared between managers of the different divisions likely to be affected: transportation or waste disposal, for example. If you have a legal department, give it final responsibility for keeping track of regulations that affect your operations.

The information you are gathering is often local or regional, but it is also part of the larger North American context. Environmental laws are often complex in design, but their overall intent is straightforward: to reduce the negative impact of processes and products on the environment. Most have been passed in order to restrict or prohibit activities that are seen as harmful to health and the environment. As such, they are often punitive and costly for business to implement, frequently requiring a sizable capital investment. However, a different type of environmental legislation is emerging, which is based on the incentive model. These are legislative "carrots" designed to encourage, through the use of measures such as tax credits, practices that are cleaner and greener. In the long run, we predict that various forms of incentives and disincentives will largely displace the current complex array of restrictive regulations.

Two decades ago, when most countries established environmental ministries or agencies, the initial spate of regulations was described as "react and cure" legislation. Many of these laws still govern business operations today. The United States Clean Air Act, which became law in 1970, is an example of the kind of punitive legislation to which governments have traditionally resorted. An updated version of this Act was signed into law by President George Bush at the end of 1990. Although this new legislation contains some incentives, it is mostly punitive, and already U.S. industry is saying that it will cost US$25 billion annually by the end of the decade. Among other provisions, the new law will force oil companies to cut toxic refinery emissions by as much as 90 percent, and to develop cleaner-burning fuels for smog-choked urban areas. It will also regulate 191 toxic chemicals (compared to the 7 that have been on the books since 1970) and require power plants to cut total nationwide sulfur dioxide emissions (the main cause of acid rain) by five million tons by 1995 and by an additional ten million tons by the year 2000.

"There's no doubt that there are sizable economic costs," says Dale Jorgenson, a Harvard University economics professor, "especially for the industries that are directly impacted, like electric utilities and autos." The tough new Act is a clear indication that government has the will to enforce environmental standards, and that the public is demanding it. In fact, it is even tougher than the version sent to Congress by President Bush, allowing him to make good on his promise to be the first environmental president. The largest companies in the United States will be hardest hit and are already lobbying the Environmental Protection Agency (EPA), which is charged with writing the regulations that the *Wall Street Journal* says will, "by the choice of a few words, make millions of dollars of difference to polluters."

The Act will also affect small businesses, including some never before regulated, forcing them to share in the clean-up costs traditionally assumed by large companies. The list of potential impacts is lengthy: jobs may be lost (in polluting industries forced to close down), consumer products may have to be reformulated, services such as dry cleaning will cost more and consumers will absorb hefty hikes in energy, automobile and gasoline costs as both cars and fuels are required to be cleaner.

Why the push now for tougher regulations? Green voter pressure and a growing body of scientific evidence of environmental problems are the two most common reasons cited. The American and Canadian regulatory pictures differ slightly—the U.S. is tougher than Canada on most issues—but neither country has a strong record of enforcement. Regardless of whether new legislation continues to be introduced, existing legislation will be strengthened in both countries, and again the American experience is telling. The EPA is now at the Cabinet level, leading most observers to believe that new get-tough policies will be enforced, in stark contrast to the record of the past twenty years.

Canada's Environmental Protection Act of 1989 includes equally stringent pollution-control measures, and provisions for enforcement. The Act aims to prevent environmental problems before they occur, by imposing controls on toxic substances throughout their full life cycle, regulating fuels and fuel components, emissions and effluents, waste handling and disposal practices, air pollution, and dumping at sea. It requires companies to take measures to prevent industrial accidents, and under the new law polluters may be fined up to CDN$1 million a day. Corporate officials can also be charged for authorizing or participating in violation of the Act. Observers say that by the middle of this decade as free trade is more fully realized, the two countries' systems will be rationalized. Meanwhile, the trend toward tougher laws will continue.

During this same time period provincial and state regulations are expected to increase in number, particularly with regard to local issues. New legislation aimed at limiting solid waste and reducing the harmful impact of products and materials is already proliferating at the regional level. While some insiders believe that there will be a continued transfer of regulatory responsibility from the federal to the local level, Canada's Bill C-78, which is expected to be passed in 1991, is an exception to this trend. The bill establishes a federal environmental assessment process that will override provincial jurisdiction "in circumstances where those impacts would be likely to be serious," as the bill itself says. It would also require environmental impact assessments for all major projects under federal jurisdiction, although it includes provisions for mediation, so that a tailored solution can be developed.

While most of these new regulations remain restrictive and punitive, various types of incentives are now beginning to appear. This trend is reassuring, since incentives encourage innovation by working with the market, rather than against it. There are two primary types of market-based incentives with which business must currently contend: emission rights and tax schemes. Emission rights, or tradable credits schemes, allow the trading of pollution "rights" or "credits" within a specified jurisdiction. Here is how the scheme works. The government establishes acceptable emission levels for various pollutants within a given region. Each company operating in that area is allowed to pollute up to that level. However, if the builders of new Factory A find it economically feasible to incorporate technologies that reduce its emission levels to *below* the permitted level, it can then sell its "spare polluting capacity" to Factory B, which is currently exceeding the limits. Factory B is an older generating station that is going to be phased out in a few years and finds it cheaper to purchase Factory A's pollution credits than to invest in new equipment. When averaged out between Factory A and B, the overall pollution ceiling is still met, and each company is able to achieve its goal in the most economical way. The new U.S. Clean Air Act includes provisions for such a scheme in its acid rain category, but the idea has been in practice in a handful of regions in the United States since the 1970s.

Other incentive programs, which are sometimes referred to as "disincentives," include taxes or fees paid on polluting goods, an example of internalizing at least some of the environmental cost, a fundamental tenet of geonomics. Producers and importers of CFCs, for example, pay an escalating price per pound fee and the revenue from the "taxes" is used to spur research for alternative products. The U.S. government estimates that environmental tax revenues over the next five years could total as much as $20 billion for sulfur dioxide and nitrogen oxide emissions alone, and grants for research and development of cleaner technology—including recycling operations—will become more commonplace.

Some companies are fighting not only these innovations, but all environmental legislation. They fear that regulations will limit their plans for expansion, and state that all regulations are too expensive. The greenest firms believe that if industry wants flexibility in determining solutions to environmental problems, it must be perceived as being willing to shoulder its share of responsibility. They note further that if the newest form of regulations—market-based incentives—fails, command-and-control regulations will be around for a long time. Not only do these regulations not work today, opponents argue, they were never all that effective. For example, the original U.S. Clean Air Act required coal-burning facilities to have tall chimneys, which removed the problem from one area, but compounded it in another.

Many companies that operate in the industrialized nations are now spending staggering amounts on pollution control in order to meet increasingly stringent standards. Bayer AG, the German chemical company, has revealed that it spends the same amount on environmental protection as it does on labor and energy—about twenty cents on every dollar. Because of the new Clean Air Act, American oil giant Chevron expects environmental spending to grow by 10 percent a year. So if you are in an industry where pollution is a problem, a sensible green corporate strategy would include the goal of having your company clean up in advance of and better than your competitors.

The challenge for government is to create a regulatory climate that stimulates new ideas and nurtures technological creativity, but doesn't simply freeze the development process at a technology level that is only slightly cleaner than the one being banned. Business analysts believe that the recent U.S. electoral defeat of a number of new environmental regulations, such as California's "Big Green," sends a message to government: the public wants legislation that is specific, easy to understand and cost-effective. The next Big Green may not be quite as big or as green, but it will come sooner or later. The public will continue to demand that pollution be reduced and polluters punished, that packaging be reduced and be recyclable, that products be less harmful in the making and the disposing.

Given this situation, your green strategy will have to be tailored to your specific industry and the types of regulations you can foresee. But you also need to adopt a strategy toward the whole regulatory process: are you going to fight it, grudgingly go along with it or keep ahead of it? The greenest companies have chosen the latter option. "Our job is to do it our way, before we have a sword hanging over our heads," says Richard J. Mahoney, CEO of Monsanto Chemical Company. Monsanto and many other companies are working to clean up their own acts before the government forces them to.

There is much more to this than good public relations. The success of the Montreal Protocol (which calls for a global reduction in the use of CFCs) is largely dependent on industry support. Du Pont, the largest manufacturer of CFCs in the world, not only supported the protocol, but announced that it would exceed its stipulations. Some observers said that this was because of the concerns of Du Pont and other larger users about liability, the fear that contributors to the ozone layer's thinning would face lawsuits from people who develop skin cancer. But maybe something much more interesting was also going on. Du Pont was pushing governments to give money to developing nations to help find alternatives to polluting technology and chemicals such as CFCs. Some of that money, not surprisingly, will go to Du Pont operations in Mexico and Brazil, which are already working on solving these problems. This is an excellent example of the potential rewards for companies who act rather than wait to react.

Companies are also cooperating with government and advocacy groups to develop regulations that are workable and still meet the needs of all parties. This new approach has been dubbed regulation-negotiation or "reg-neg." In contrast to the old regulations, the new laws can be categorized as those which "anticipate and prevent." Regulation redesigners know that getting industry to use the cleanest technology for the lowest cost is the optimum goal.

So what signals does all this send to a company that wishes to formulate a green strategy? For one thing, it means that if you are not already monitoring what's happening in your jurisdiction and elsewhere, then you will almost certainly be caught off guard. We believe it also means that you would be well advised to become more involved in such negotiations and to try to influence regulations in your favor, or at least ensure they are balanced. Some industries are lobbying to postpone or weaken environmental measures, but it would seem that the smarter course is to cooperate with regulators and work with other interested groups in the designing of workable solutions that satisfy all parties—including the moderate environmentalist lobbies—and then aim to generously exceed them. That way, when the next round of regulations is on the drawing board, you will be positioned to argue for even stricter rules that will make you more competitive.

Monitor Changing Product Standards

Whether you are ahead of the legislation or not, greening your products and services will put them in a more favorable competitive position. In North America today this greening can be as straightforward as changing a single element in your product's content or packaging, thereby making it greener than those of your competitors. But while such changes can be a great marketplace differentiator, it soon won't be enough. As part of your ongoing intelligence gathering it pays to monitor emerging environmental product standards.

One of the most significant recent developments in this area has been a standardized green product approval system, known as eco-labeling. Eco-labeling programs are administered by a national agency that has been established for this express purpose. The schemes set out a precise series of environmental criteria that a product must meet in order to be awarded with a green seal of approval, ranging from how it is manufactured to how much energy it requires to operate and how it is disposed of. Eco-labeling is intended to provide information that will assist consumers in deciding which goods in the marketplace have a reduced impact on the environment. Most schemes are strictly comparative—product A is better than product B—and recognize technology that is better rather than best. While the programs are largely targeted toward consumers, considerable interest has also been expressed by companies that sell to other businesses.

To apply for an eco-label, a manufacturer will submit a product to the co-ordinating organization. The product is then assessed according to established criteria for its product category and submitted to a lengthy and detailed testing procedure; in most countries this cost is borne by the manufacturer. Once the product has been approved, it is awarded with an eco-label logo that generally includes a description of why the product has been approved. The manufacturer may use this logo on the product's label and in any advertising.

The first eco-labels appeared in West Germany in 1978. Since then the idea has spread and by 1990 Canada, Japan and Norway had launched their own programs and many others were in the planning stages; all are based on the West German prototype. West Germany's voluntary program was quickly embraced by manufacturers, who recognized that in a marketplace driven by green consumers it was in their own interest to carry such certification. To date more than three thousand products in fifty-five categories carry West Germany's Blue Angel symbol.

Opinion surveys across Europe indicate strong consumer support for eco-labeling and the European Community is developing a program that will apply to all its members. An international scheme is likely to emerge later this decade, aimed at preventing eco-labeling from becoming a serious trade barrier. It is already affecting North American exports to West Germany where manufacturers are finding it difficult to sell products not carrying the Blue Angel logo or labeled under a different system.

In the United States, three competing schemes are currently underway: a government-sponsored program (still in the planning stages, this could be administered by the EPA), and two private programs, Green Seal and Green Cross. So far, American manufacturers have been cautious or disinterested, but this could change quickly. All it will take, as in the German example, is for one or two major companies to apply for certification under a program and everyone else will have to follow suit. We recommend that you investigate these programs and that you submit your appropriate products for approval. Ultimately, the strict criteria of eco-labeling schemes will determine what goes into a product before it reaches the marketplace, so the more you know about them now, the better.

In the course of developing your green business strategy, it is wise to research existing or emerging labeling standards, including eco-labeling programs. Their impact on the goods and services you sell cannot be ignored. For example, products will be deemed ungreen if they don't carry the green seal of approval. Manufacturers have the right of appeal, but both the approval and the appeal process are lengthy and expensive; far better to get it right the first time around. Eco-labeling will also be able to help you identify the emerging environmental issues that affect your business: each product category has been specifically researched for its "environmental burden." We review the product-development aspect of eco-labeling in more detail in

Chapter Five, but emphasize here that the emergence of green product and service standards will have a powerful impact on the kinds of products and services you develop, whether you sell to consumers or to other businesses.

Take a Hard Look at Your Environmental Liability

No corporate green strategy is complete without some provision for reducing environmental risk. In North America today, liability for the damage caused by pollution and for the cost of environmental clean-up extends far beyond the traditional limits: it can even apply to a site you no longer own and to practices that were perfectly legal at the time you used them. In addition, the cost of breaking environmental regulations is rising rapidly. In 1989 indictments and convictions for the infringement of environmental laws in the United States were double that of the previous year, with US$13 million in fines levied. And the long arm of the law is reaching into the executive suite, as dozens of corporate directors and officers have been held personally responsible, and sometimes jailed, for their companies' transgressions. In 1989, prison sentences totaling thirty-seven years were handed out to U.S. executives whose companies contravened environmental legislation. Although Canada has been slower to prosecute executives, in 1990 the owner of an Ontario firm was jailed for six months for knowingly releasing toxic effluent into the Don River.

Perhaps the main reason to assess your environmental liability is the skyrocketing cost of industrial accidents. The spill at Union Carbide's plant in Bhopal, India, in 1984 was more expensive than previous, similar accidents, primarily because civil class action lawsuits were launched that forced the company to pay large personal injury and damage claim settlements. However, after Bhopal, the accident that has most frightened business and alerted insurers was the *Exxon Valdez* spill off the Alaskan coast in 1989. Although the accident was not nearly as serious as the *Amoco Cadiz* spill a decade earlier, the price Exxon paid was much higher. The *Exxon Valdez* spilled only 16 percent as much oil but paid seventeen times the amount Amoco did to clean it up—US$2 billion. Further, the combination of public outrage, consumer backlash and a harsh response from regulators has proved to be much more punishing. Exxon is still recovering.

We are only beginning to understand the extent to which companies will be held liable for environmental damage they have already caused, are causing today or will cause in the future. Doing the minimum to forestall liability creates a time bomb. "Those who live by the regulations, and who believe they will solve all their problems, hold an extremely naive view," says Alcan Aluminum director of environmental affairs, Dr. Raymond Brouzes. "There was a PCB example in New York State that I think sums this up rather well. The government said, 'Yes, this waste disposal site is licenced—it's okay to dump here.' But five years later, it was found that the dumpsite owner pumped toxic waste into the groundwater, and all of the companies who dumped there have been held liable. Having a permit is no guarantee. We need to take cradle-to-grave responsibility for our products."

Trying to determine such long-term liability is a significant challenge. The unknown future of manufacturing processes, construction materials and by-products now presents an increasing element of environmental risk. "As the science of the environment becomes more sophisticated, society is going to find some interesting things with respect to bioaccumulation [the accumulation of chemicals in biological matter]," says E.F. Boswell, president of E.B. Eddy Forest Products Limited. "We don't yet understand the full implications of chemicals in the food chain, and we must concentrate more research in that area. I guarantee there will be an attempt to determine liability for these things in the not-too-distant future."

As a result of this trend, some companies are demanding that the contracts they sign detail all identifiable environmental assets and liabilities and that future liability be determined before a product or a property changes hands. When Nova Corp. of Calgary sold its synthetic rubber division to Bayer AG of West Germany for CDN$1.25 billion, the deal included $230 million for debt and other liabilities, including potential environmental risks such as underground storage tanks.

In a related development, new standards developed by chartered accounting organizations require a company's environmental liabilities to be shown as dollar liabilities on their books and in their annual reports, another example of geonomics at work. Or to take a simple example, the owner of a building containing asbestos would have to write down its value based on the cost of removing this environmental hazard. Preventive measures such as the removal of toxic substances, though usually costly, are a bargain compared to the cost of cleaning up spills or leaks. In our opinion such cost-avoidance measures are the best bet for business.

A prime example of the lengths to which companies will now go to minimize environmental risks can be found in Oakville, Ontario, where Shell Canada Limited is preparing a former refinery site for residential and commercial use. In what is proving to be a test case in the development of government guidelines for such projects, Shell is investing more than CDN$13 million to clean up the site. But the company considers this expenditure necessary to protect itself against future damage claims. In sum, you can't be too rigorous in your attempts to minimize risk.

Liability Insurance

If you haven't talked to your insurance company about what all this is going to mean for next year's premiums or the next policy you negotiate, do it immediately. Insurers are becoming increasingly uncomfortable about providing coverage for environmental damage. As a result, the cost of corporate liability insurance is going to escalate dramatically for companies involved in risk-prone endeavors. Even when insurance is available, many companies have concluded that their coverage is inadequate. After the *Exxon Valdez* spill, U.S. shipping firms increased their insurance coverage from the standard liability range of US$100–150 million to US$750 million. One oil company, Shell, decided that the problems associated with getting US$1 billion-plus pollution-risk coverage were too high, and announced it will no longer ship to most U.S. ports.

Property/casualty insurers say that they can no longer be passive in their usual role as risk assessors and underwriters. Beyond their responsibility to shareholders, they have a responsibility to ensure that their prevention and control rules are tightened. Otherwise, they may face claims of billions of dollars for environmental clean-up. "Insurers will become increasingly reluctant to insure polluters," says Roy Elms, Chairman of the Insurance Bureau of Canada, "because the potential exposure is enormous, and liability is often slow to emerge." Elms believes that business has to exercise great vigilance and that if companies can't get coverage, they shouldn't be operating—a sentiment echoed throughout the industry. Some European and Canadian insurers are drafting liability insurance policies that exclude pollution coverage. Environmental liability is a separate policy, and a very expensive one.

Insiders say that the next step for the insurance industry will likely be a code of environmental principles with which all clients will have to comply. "The bottom line," according to independent insurance adjuster and consultant, Steve Sobel, "is that the insurance industry no longer wants to be used as a safety net. This cannot continue. In the Exxon case, they were in dangerous waters. They knew the risks, and our industry should have asked the questions, but no one did. The end result is that insurers will be reluctant to insure polluters, or may refuse to pay the claim, in the belief that the polluters knew what they were doing."

If you are in a business that takes environmental risks—and most businesses do—then your corporate green strategy ought to include a plan for reducing those risks wherever possible. The problems include the following: heavy government fines for breaking environmental regulations, legal liability for environmental damage and jail terms for your executives.

You have several options. Some companies are attempting to organize cooperative insurance in order to reduce premiums or simply make it possible to get insurance for their activities. "Risk Retention Groups," as they are known in industry, allow companies to pay for their own losses out of a reserve fund designed for this purpose. A U.S. insurance industry executive recently admitted that as many as one-third of the premiums formerly paid to insurance companies are now handled in this manner. But this is a stopgap measure.

In the long run, it is most effective to make your company less of an environmental risk by cleaning up every aspect of your operation, a process we describe in detail in Chapter Four. The majority of green pioneers have taken this route. Not only does it reduce their annual insurance bills, it gives them a defence in the event that something does go wrong. U.S. and Canadian courts are beginning to recognize the defence of "due diligence" or "reasonable care" in cases of prosecution for environmental damage. If a company can show that it has done everything that could reasonably be expected of it in making its practices environmentally safe, then the charges are often dismissed, or the sentencing reduced in severity.

In sum, a smart green strategy is based on a careful analysis of not only the benefits of going green, but the risks of not doing so. One of the chief ways of measuring your environmental risk is to commission an environmental audit of your operations, a subject we also cover in detail in Chapter Four.

Talk to Your Banker about Financing

Increasingly, financial institutions are considering the environmental impact of their credit and investment decisions. Many bankers are now demanding environmental assessments before granting loans. Sizable environmental risks will increasingly translate into higher costs for the borrower and may impair that borrower's credit rating. If the level of environmental risk is deemed to be unreasonably high, credit may simply not be extended.

David L. Robertson, senior vice-president, corporate banking, at The Royal Bank of Canada, Canada's largest and North America's third-largest financial institution, describes what a bank might typically face in a high-risk situation. "A borrowing company is forced to incur added environmental costs for fines, clean-ups or increased waste disposal, may encounter cash flow difficulties, and be unable to service its bank debt. In some cases, the survival of the business may even be threatened, and if the loan is secured by property affected by pollution, the value of that security may be severely damaged." As this sort of thing happens more frequently, lenders will become increasingly cautious and will examine more carefully the environmental implications of their actions.

Banks are also worried about being stuck with third-party liability. This is where the owner or party in financial control of the property (often a financial institution) is held responsible for environmental damages and clean-up, even though these are the result of someone else's negligence. "There have been a few highly publicized such cases in the U.S.," Robertson comments, "although one has not yet happened in Canada. One that comes to mind involved the Maryland Bank and Trust Company, which made a loan of $335,000 to a company on which it eventually had to foreclose. The bank took over the company, only to find that its property was contaminated. It cost the bank $500,000, considerably more than the original loan, in subsequent clean-up costs."

As a result of these developments, your next loan application will likely have to leap a few environmental hurdles. It is now standard practice, for example, for financial institution account managers to follow a set of environmental guidelines when appraising your funding request. Should something in your proposal be on their checklist of red-flag issues (such as redevelopment of industrial land), they will call in an environmental expert and order an assessment at your expense. Issues now routinely reviewed with borrowers include environmental regulations, hazardous waste generation and the ability to pay for clean-ups and third-party damages.

There is a positive side to this story, however. If you are looking for financing for a new green business, such as environmental consulting or green product manufacturing, you will likely find money easier to borrow. The banks are targeting these areas as growth industries with better-than-average profit potential and they want them in their investment portfolios. In essence, the companies that are cleanest and greenest are also those most likely to experience preferred status when borrowing funds.

Watch for Emerging Business Opportunites

New business opportunities may not be your motivation for going green—you may simply want to bring your company's standards up to the levels demanded in the 1990s—but as you begin the greening process you may discover unexpected new business opportunities. One of the best examples of this is Du Pont's move into the environmental clean-up business. The chemical company developed products and processes to clean up its own operations, then discovered that it could offset these costs by selling this technology to other firms. Du Pont now expects that this new division will generate US$1 billion in business during the 1990s.

Companies involved in the production of green goods and services are experiencing a tremendous growth rate, as much as four times the annual average. Of this broad spectrum of new business opportunities, the environmental protection sector shows the most potential. Several hundred firms active in waste management, pollution control, environmental clean-up and environmental engineering have been launched in North America and Europe in the last two years, and literally dozens more will come on stream in 1991. Smaller companies and European-based firms seem to be leading the way in entrepreneurial imagination, but we expect that larger North American companies will follow Du Pont's successful lead and introduce new divisions to capitalize on the growing demand.

In the United States, companies that are already producing green products such as low-sulfur coal are experiencing a sharp increase in demand for this environmentally-improved fuel. Many of the jobs and profits from polluting industries are moving to companies that make cleaner products and services, or that help clean up other firms' environmental problems. Such companies are experiencing such an upsurge in demand for their services that they can't keep up.

As you move through the process of greening, new business opportunities will undoubtedly emerge, in the form of markets for products you require for your own clean-up, for green versions of your existing goods or for services you can offer to help other companies go green.

Talk To The Environmental Experts

As we suggested in the introduction to this chapter, much of the information you need to develop a green business strategy will come from sources you would not have been aware of even a few years ago. For example, business is increasingly discovering that environmental organizations have information and expertise they need. These groups can be an excellent source of environmental intelligence and of the innovative ideas that are required to meet the demands of a changing marketplace, such as the development of green products and programs, as was the case with Loblaws. We are including environmental consultants in this section as well. While many of them do not have backgrounds as environmentalists, these self-made environmental experts must maintain a network of contacts with green groups in order to be most effective.

Environmental Groups

"My first encounter with environmentalists in Loblaws' boardroom was enlightening," Patrick recalls. "We invited the representatives of several groups to meet with us at our offices. My assistant seated them in the boardroom along with our research staff and when I came in I was taken aback. 'Where are the ponytails and the t-shirts?' I wondered. I wouldn't have been able to distinguish these environmentalists from Wall Street brokers."

Patrick's anecdote illustrates one of the common misconceptions many business people have: that environmentalists are still mired in more radical days. In fact, their organizations are often run by staff and volunteers with law degrees, MBAs and PhDs. These people are experts at lobbying, raising money and influencing public opinion. Environmentalism is a very different quantity than it was twenty years ago. While some groups are still radical, and would like to see free market capitalism disbanded, most are moderate and willing to work with business to green the marketplace. Just as business is beginning to recognize the value of co-operation in achieving its goals, most environmentalists realize that significant gains can be made by working within the system. Many mainstream groups are now in favor of developing alliances with business. This changed attitude is aptly expressed by Bryn James, former Greenpeace chairperson and now managing director of Landbank Consultancy, a U.K. environmental consulting firm. "Because our problems are caused by industry, the solutions must be defined by industry. Environmentalists have got to roll up their sleeves and get to work with industry. There's no point standing on the sidelines shrieking abuse."

The majority of modern environmental groups came to life in the radical sixties in response to public concerns about polluting industries, waste disposal siting and other high-profile environmental issues. Some, particularly conservationist organizations, have been around much longer. The Sierra Club, for one, has been in existence since the turn of the century. In the last two decades the newest green groups have played a significant role in opposing what they believe are potentially harmful developments and in publicizing the latest research about modern society's growing impact on the natural environment. Until recently, the relationship between contemporary environmental organizations and business has been characterized for the most part by public confrontation. But as we now know, things have progressed a long way in a very few years. We review some of the promising new alliances later in this section.

We recommend that one of the best ways you can monitor the evolving environmental agenda is by exploring the possibility of establishing contact with, or even an alliance with, an environmental organization. Before you do this, however, it is important to understand the differences between the major organizations so that you can approach them intelligently. What are their objectives? How do they raise funds? Which ones work with business? Are there any who remain—despite the trend toward bridge-building—the enemy? Although you will find it easier to work with the moderate environmental groups, it is helpful to have an understanding of the whole spectrum of green groups. The chart on page 44 shows a cross section of North American groups as of the beginning of 1991.

Although this survey of forty well-known environmental organizations is relatively small, it covers the many variations on environmental thought that exist in the early 1990s. The continuum ranges from activist groups like Earth First to environmental research organizations like Energy Probe. In between, the spectrum includes the more moderate advocacy organizations such as the Council on Economic Priorities, mainstream, often well-established conservationist organizations

	North American Organizations	U.S. Organizations	Canadian Organizations
Green Think Tanks		• Environmental Defense Fund (EDF) • Resources for the Future • Rocky Mountain Institute (RMI) • World Resources Institute (WRI) • Worldwatch Institute	• Energy Probe
Educational Policy-Setting	• Atlantic Centre for the Environment • Canada-United States Environmental Council	• Climate Institute • John Muir Institute for Environmental Studies • Wildlife Habitat Enhancement Council • World Environment Center • The Conservation Foundation	• Canadian Arctic Resources Committee • Harmony Foundation
Conservationist	• Ducks Unlimited • Sierra Club • Wildlife Federation • World Wildlife Fund (WWF)	• Anglers for Clean Water • Audubon Society	• Canadian Nature Federation • Canadian Wildlife Federation • The Nature Conservancy of Canada
Advocacy	• Acid Rain Foundation	• Conservation Law Foundation (CLF) • Council on Economic Priorities (CEP) • Cultural Survival • Natural Resources Defense Council (NRDC) • The Windstar Foundation	• Canadian Environmental Law Association (CELA) • Pollution Probe
Activist	• Earth First • Friends of the Earth (FoE) • Greenpeace	• Clean Water Action • Defenders of Wildlife • Rainforest Action Network • Treepeople	

like the Sierra Club, and groups whose primary focus is the development of alliances between organizations as an environmental-protection strategy. In general, their philosophies can be categorized as either: (1) calling for radical social change or (2) looking for improvements within existing social structures.

The chart lists major environmental organizations, but there are literally thousands of others across North America that we don't mention here. These largely unsung groups—everything from environmental foundations, scientific groups, professional associations and regional groups to the obscure organizations, such as TRAFFIC—Trade Records Analysis for Flora and Fauna in Commerce, which monitors trade in wild and endangered species, are also doing important, often community-based work on green concerns.

The level of public interest in environmental issues, and the growing support for green groups must not be underestimated. In 1989 *Time* magazine reported that membership in environmental groups worldwide had risen from 13.3 million in 1988 to 15.9 million. Other sources put the numbers in the hundreds of millions. When you consider everything from a North American NIMBY to independent development organizations in Third World countries, this figure may be more accurate. We believe that the numbers are at an all time high, and will continue to climb. Cambridge Reports, the Massachusetts pollsters, say that 14 percent of the American population is involved in some way in environmental activism, even if it is just a matter of sending a donation.

As we mentioned earlier, there has been an impressive leap in the credibility of environmental organizations, particularly in the last three years. But no matter how much they may be willing to ally themselves with business, it is important to keep in mind that most green groups are different in many ways and will remain so. Often there are important differences in management style. Some environmental organizations are non-hierarchical, and make decisions by consensus. Some even ignore traditional models completely by paying all of their staff the same salary, regardless of position or experience. In addition, some of these groups are federations with large numbers of regional offices or chapters, each with its own objective. Don't assume that the understanding you come to with a local group will be shared across the country.

In addition to working to protect the environment, these groups put a great deal of effort and energy into fundraising to finance their operations and projects. In fact, some critics predict that the larger the organizations get, the more time they will have to spend raising money, thus deflecting their attention away from their larger purpose. The phenomenal growth in membership that some of these organizations have experienced over the past two years threatens to overwhelm them, and many groups are scrambling to put new management systems into place that will help them cope with their increasing popularity.

As alliances with business begin to develop on a more regular basis, some of the groups have divided themselves into two administrative parts: the first charitable, and the second revenue-generating. The for-profit division meets two objectives: it allows the group to act as a consultant and to charge for its services without jeopardizing the non-profit status of the other division, and it is also run more like a traditional business, allowing it to function more effectively in the corporate sector. Over time, mainstream environmental organizations will begin to establish stronger financial bases. For now, many are on a shaky footing, dependent on the success of the latest direct mail campaign to meet the monthly payroll.

In the remainder of this section we characterize a number of these groups, with a particular emphasis on their record of corporate alliances. For an annotated listing of the major North American groups most likely to work with business, please see Appendix 2.

Green Think Tanks

The central objective of green think tanks is to research emerging environmental issues. Each organization manages this task in a different way: some provide crucial and accurate information to policy-makers, while others work to develop marketplace applications for their ideas. Much of the information they provide and the ideas they generate were once considered radical, but have recently moved into our mainstream practices. An example of a formerly fringe idea that is now common in business circles is zero discharge as an emissions objective for industry.

Two organizations typify the work being done in these circles. The Rocky Mountain Institute (RMI) is an independent foundation with a primary focus on the development of energy-efficiency models. By early 1991, RMI had worked with 160 utilities across North America. Close to a hundred organizations, including Westinghouse, Ciba-Geigy and Phillips Petroleum, subscribe to its COMPETITEK service, which features detailed information on how to save electricity. Founders Amory and Hunter Lovins say that cost-effective energy management can radically reduce the burden on the environment and have a positive impact on the bottom line as well.

The New York-based Environmental Defense Fund (EDF) recently scored two important successes. In 1990 it announced the formation of a joint task force with McDonald's that will identify new ways to reduce the trash generated by the company's 11,000 restaurants worldwide. The task force is an excellent example of the kind of alliance that works best. The objective is focused and there is a fixed timeframe. The Fund's innovative partnership of environmental science, law, economics and computer science also helped it develop an economic model for environmental control that became part of the new U.S. Clean Air Act.

Green think tank funding comes from donations, services, government and business.

Educational/Policy-Setting Organizations

Educational and alliance-building organizations work in a steady and regular way to educate the public, professionals and regulators about environmental issues. Some, such as the Wildlife

Habitat Enhancement Council, were developed explicitly to bring business on side with environmental concerns. The Council encourages corporations to enhance their undeveloped lands for the benefit of wildlife, fish and plant life.

Canada's Harmony Foundation has also blazed some interesting trails with business. Most recently, it has cooperated with The Royal Bank of Canada in the development of a broad-based environmental program that involves the general public. In 1990, the bank published *Home and Family Guide: Practical Action for the Environment*, a handbook on environmental issues that includes many useful ideas about what consumers can do to green their lives.

Conservationist Organizations

Conservation organizations are generally the green groups that are most well-established and that have been around for the longest time—some since before the turn of the century. As might be expected, their focus is not explicitly "environmental" but more broadly "naturalist," and their number includes a significant hunter-angler component.

Ducks Unlimited is one of the newest entries to the field; in its work to preserve waterfowl wildlands it makes use of the most sophisticated communications and advocacy techniques. Even the organization's attention-grabbing name is a sign of changing times in the conservationist sector; it is no longer necessary to give your organization a dry name in order to be taken seriously.

This shift is further underlined by the Sierra Club's new activist stance. According to Michael Fischer, executive director of The Sierra Club USA, "If there was ever a time when aggressive grassroots environmental action was needed, it is now. The 1990s will be the pivotal decade when crucial decisions will be made about the future of our planet." The Club's Arctic National Wildlife Refuge Protection Program, for example, argues that drilling for oil in the arctic should cease. And it intends to lobby intensively to achieve this goal.

Other conservation organizations, including the World Wildlife Fund (WWF) are actively pursuing alliances with business. The WWF's Conservation Council works with educational institutions to establish programs that identify how environmental issues impact everyday business. Companies such as Dow, Du Pont and General Motors are active members, meeting regularly to discuss environmental concerns and how to integrate these concerns into corporate decision-making through the development of educational programs.

Funding comes from memberships, donations in support of specific programs; financial contributions from the corporate sector are generally welcome.

Advocacy Organizations

More than ever before these organizations are willing to work within existing structures in their quest for environmental improvements. They might be characterized as groups that lobby for greener laws, then try to make sure they are enforced.

Organizations such as the Natural Resources Defense Council (NRDC) and the Conservation Law Foundation (CLF) have lobbied business and government for years to change their polluting practices. Both now work with private utilities to design and implement energy-efficiency programs. The NRDC has been working with Pacific Gas and Electric (PG&E), the world's largest investor-owned utility with annual revenues of US$9 billion to introduce an energy-management program. As of 1990, PG&E became the world's largest private institutional investor in energy efficiency, developing partnerships with thousands of its commercial and residential customers.

Pollution Probe, the Canadian organization whose partnership with Loblaws is explored extensively in this book, is also included in this category. Founded at the University of Toronto in the 1970s over concerns about the quality of the city's drinking water, the group's mandate has broadened considerably to include acid rain, food additives and Great Lakes pollution.

Traditionally, media attention for groups such as this has been low key; Pollution Probe was able to dramatically increase its exposure during the launch of Loblaws' G.R.E.E.N line.

Harvard-based Cultural Survival is another environmental group under the advocacy banner that is doing some important work with the business sector. The organization is best known for its efforts to lobby on behalf of indigenous peoples, and has begun to import products grown on endangered lands in developing countries. As of 1991, more than twenty different companies are working with Cultural Survival, including Ben & Jerry's Homemade, Inc., the Vermont ice cream company that makes Rainforest Crunch ice cream with cashews and brazil nuts from South America.

Funding comes from membership, donations, consulting services and government grants.

Activist Organizations

These groups are known for their ability to successfully market their product—environmental activism and adventure—through adroit use of the media. They are thus able to draw attention to the environmental issues they identify as critical, and to constantly stimulate their chief source of funding, donations.

Since the late 1980s this entire category can no longer be classified as radical, although Earth First's controversial tactics are definitely beyond the fringe. In general, these organizations are more willing to develop links with government and business than at any time in their twenty-year history. In the last few years many of these organizations, particularly Greenpeace and Friends of the Earth, have stopped telling business to simply "shut down the factory," and are helping them develop more sustainable practices.

This category of environmental organizations has the most decentralized management style, and many of them refuse funding from business.

In sum, diversity has characterized all these environmental organizations since their inception, and we expect the dividing lines and the groups' objectives and strategies to become more clearly defined in the 1990s. But the companies that work to establish links with environmental organizations today will discover that the gap between "us" and "them" is often very small and can be profitably bridged.

Environmental Consultants

In addition to or in place of developing alliances with environmental organizations, we recommend that you consider hiring an environmental consultant. There are already a number of professionals in this field, and more are entering the marketplace each year. One hundred and twenty-five consulting firms were listed when the United Kingdom's Environmental Data Services published a directory of environmental advisers in 1988. Since then, the number has doubled in the U.K., and North America is not far behind.

In general terms, an environmental consultant is an individual or firm that helps you decipher environmental issues as they apply to your company, and suggests a range of strategies that will help you respond to and profit from these new demands. Some act as effective bridge-builders between environmental and corporate communities, decoding the different ideologies and structures of each. We recommend that you use environmental consultants the same way you use advisers on any other issue. Consultants can help you:

- prepare an independent, objective review of your company's current environmental performance
- design an environmental strategy that can be accomplished in stages, based on budget and staff
- develop a management system that incorporates your new, green objectives and regulatory requirements
- propose cost-reduction measures and identify new business opportunities

- communicate your company's and products' greenness to your constitutents
- develop plans to execute and monitor your overall green strategy

Of course, not all environmental consultants offer the same services or bring the same level of expertise to the table. Some are independent consultants, a number of them former environmentalists who have excellent contacts with groups and government. Others are environmental-service departments of law firms, engineering companies or accounting-management consulting firms. These organizations specialize in certain types of environmental consulting: a law firm may perform regulatory-compliance checks, an engineering firm waste-management audits or energy-efficiency analyses. While some environmental consultants restrict their work to specific industries, most have expertise that is transferable to any number of business sectors and jurisdictions.

How does a company choose a consultant from a field that includes both large firms and smaller independents? "Talk to others in your industry," says Glynn Young, manager of editorial services at Monsanto. "Word of mouth about a consultant's track record and knowledge of your industry is your best bet." Our advice is to begin by choosing an environmental consulting firm that will be able to provide your company with a broad perspective and a range of services. First identify your specific requirements, interview a number of consulting groups and ask for a written proposal with estimated costs to help you make your decision.

More than anything, consultants will help you keep the longer view in sight, so you can stay abreast of trends as they relate to your industry—everything from new solid waste laws to changing consumer preferences to federal purchasing policies. This will help you avoid focusing too much attention on a short-term green issue or overlooking a potential time bomb. Consultants help you decipher the complex issues you face now and will face as the green agenda evolves. Patrick believes consultants are here to stay, and with good reason. "They help companies leap-frog over the issues of the moment, and encourage them to focus on the direction their industry will be taking ten years from now."

Write Your Green Strategy

This chapter has provided an overview of the kinds of issues and new green realities that your company must take into account in developing its business plan for the 1990s. As you gather information relating to all these areas, you will be able to start answering the three questions we posed in the introduction to this chapter: (1) Where are we now? (2) Where do we want to/have to go? (3) How do we get there? When Loblaws began its green program in 1988, its green business strategy was straightforward: it knew it wanted to be first in its marketplace with a line of environmentally improved consumer products. Naturally, the company has different and broader objectives today, including the addition of new products to the line, and greening its entire operation. Your company's green business strategy will also expand and evolve as you become greener and as this new way of thinking becomes more entrenched in your day-to-day operations.

Once your green strategy is formulated, the next step will be to begin to implement it. For it to be successful you will need to motivate and involve your entire staff.

▫ THREE ▫

Bring Your Team On Side

Greening your corporate culture is a necessary part of developing and implementing a green business strategy. This process begins by communicating your commitment to the environment to every employee, but it cannot end there. You must also give your staff hands-on involvement. It is not enough for the CEO and a coterie of top executives to be sold on making their company more environmentally friendly. The shift must take place on every level.

Shop floor employees are often the strongest advocates of change. In fact, many of the executives we interviewed for this book admitted that the original impetus for their company's greening came from the staff who are on the front lines and involved in day-to-day operations. In short, every person on staff is a potential source of ideas—often profitable ones. The more that people feel they are part of a team effort, the more energy and creativity they will bring to planning and implementing a green strategy. Dow Chemical Company President and CEO

Frank Popoff describes himself as "one of 62,000 environmentalists in the company." This upper-echelon attitude helps explain why Dow leads its industry in corporate greening, achieving goals far beyond those believed technically possible a few years ago.

Send Out Clear Signals

As you begin the process of greening your corporate culture, it is crucial to send out an early signal to every employee that you mean business. The clearest signal a company can send is the appointment of an environmental vice-president with real authority. Whatever you call this position, whether vice-president of health, safety and the environment, or vice-president of environmental affairs, make sure the new appointee has power, not just an impressive title. Such appointments are already an important trend, as was recently noted by John Godfrey, editor of *The Financial Post.* "Whereas once the person responsible for environmental matters was a clean-up guy—either public relations or maintenance—now there's often a vice-president in charge of the environment who works closely with the CEO and helps set strategy for the company."

The U.S. National Association of Environmental Professionals reports that their membership roster now exceeds 2,300. In the past two years, membership has trebled and nearly half of the current number are in management, with 24 percent occupying president, vice president or director positions in government agencies, private firms and consulting companies. While senior environmental positions are limited for the most part to large resource-sector firms, Loblaws, Procter & Gamble and other companies that sell directly to the consumer are recognizing the importance of having an experienced executive dedicated to environmental matters. Outside these sectors companies have been slow to add environmental departments to their organizational structure, preferring to rely on outside consultants or to make the environment one of the several responsibilities of a senior executive. In companies where a vice-president has been appointed to deal with environmental affairs, that executive's responsibilities are far-reaching. He or she will act as a liaison between the company and community, government and special interest groups, following new developments, emerging trends and consumer preferences, and representing the company's perspective in all such interactions.

By the mid-1990s it will likely be difficult to find a company that doesn't have a green-titled executive on staff. Again, we refer to Dow Chemical, who recently promoted David Buzzelli, a Canadian executive who has generated a significant amount of public interest in corporate greening, to the position of vice-president for environment, health and safety. Buzzelli's newly created department is international in scope, and he reports directly to worldwide CEO Frank Popoff.

If your environmental executive doesn't sit on the board of directors, then it is a good idea to give a board member an environmental portfolio, so that the board will be constantly reminded of the green angle to every decision. Surprisingly, senior executives remain woefully ignorant in this area. A survey conducted in England in 1989 asked two hundred senior corporate leaders what percentage of the population they believed would factor environmental issues into their purchasing decisions. The executives guessed 27 percent, while the actual figure identified earlier that year by the polling firm MORI was closer to 42 percent. Interestingly, 65 percent of these same businesspeople said they themselves would have selected one product over another because of an environmentally friendly formulation, package or advertising campaign. Appointing a green vice-president is a first step toward getting your top executives to think differently.

However, these days no CEO can afford to delegate all environmental responsibility to one vice-president. Most CEOs determine that having the environment vice-president report directly to them is an excellent way to keep a finger on the public pulse and to keep track of environmental issues and regulatory trends, but many also realize this isn't enough. To successfully guide a corporation into a greener future, CEOs will soon need to have direct experience with environmental issues. The résumés of many successful chief executives will have to include items such as "experience working with environmental groups." Already several North American companies have green commanders. The current chairman of Geneva Steel, for example, is Joe Canon, a forty-year-old former EPA regulator. When he took over as chairman, he quickly made it clear that he was serious about the environment, and his attitude spurred the development of an employee-designed solution to a chronic steel industry environmental problem: emissions from coke ovens. His own foundry workers suggested a way of redesigning the oven doors so that they now emit less than 25 percent of the regulated maximum. This shows how a clear commitment from the top can have a significant impact on front-line staff, which in turn can lead to improved operations. We advise all senior executives to do some self-education on environmental issues to show that their company's greening reflects a personal commitment to action as well.

As soon as the greening of the executive suite gets underway, communicate your new commitment and the green business strategy you are developing directly to your staff. There are many ways to do this, including simply sending your employees a letter. In 1990, AT&T's President and CEO Robert Allen published an open letter to the men and women of the company, urging employees at all levels to bring environmental awareness to bear on their daily work. Here is an excerpt: "We're setting ambitious new goals for our business," he wrote, "goals that go well beyond the requirements of government agencies .... Reaching these targets will require the attention and participation of each of us. In some cases, attainment will require technical breakthroughs and the focused attention of our best engineers and scientists. There will also be a requirement for investment. But, we are regularly reminded, up-front investment in quality pays for itself, over and over again .... I extend my thanks to those of you who have already applied your imagination and creativity to our environmental challenges. I urge each of you to consider how your actions, at home and at work, affect the environment."

Of course, mere words won't convince anyone, unless they are backed up by concrete action. Reinforce your words with in-house environmental programs to stimulate staff interest and participation. Patrick believes it is a good idea to begin with a project that mirrors what staff might already be doing in their own lives. "These are the same people who are recycling their own newspapers and pop cans. They want to know that their plant or office is as responsible as they're trying to be at home." The most effective waste management and energy conservation programs are those that give individuals a real sense they are making a difference. At this early stage it doesn't matter so much what area you zero in on. Just make sure you do something to which employees can make a visible contribution.

One excellent place to start is the staff cafeteria. In 1989 Quaker Oats of Canada Ltd. eliminated polystyrene cups by purchasing reusable ceramic cups and a dishwasher for their Peterborough, Ontario employees. In the first year, the cafeteria actually saved CDN$6,000. Such a saving was, the company admits, a bit of a surprise, but the real impact of this single move was discovered in the days that followed. "The success of our cafeteria switch had a double impact," says President Jon Grant. "Our senior management team realized that there might well be significant financial advantages to greening, and employees were encouraged to make suggestions as to how our company might change other standard practices."

How to Green Your Corporate Culture

Appointing a vice-president of the environment and setting up an in-house environmental program are really the first steps in the greening of your corporate culture. The next step is to advise your employees that you are embarking on a major research program that will lead to more environmentally friendly operations, and to the manufacture of greener products and services. Encourage their participation and ask for their ideas. Make resources and publications available to everyone and underwrite their participation in green business conferences. Emphasize that contributions from nonengineering or scientific staff are welcome and that environmental issues are relevant to all departments. Encourage your managers to work in a wide variety of areas so everyone has exposure to and experience with environmental issues.

According to Dow, it was just this kind of varied managerial background that made its waste reduction program work. Dow discovered that pollution problems can be solved in part by tapping existing expertise, such as that of plant managers, to develop solutions. In short, develop what Pacific Gas and Electric CEO Richard Clarke calls "an internal cadre of environmentalists. They have minds of their own, and will advocate things." Margaret Kerr, vice-president of environment, health and safety at Northern Telecom Limited, says employees of the electronics giant are embracing greening wholeheartedly. "Employee action really had not started until our CFC-reduction program got underway," says Kerr, "then it took off. It was like Eastern Europe. Nobody could stop it if they wanted to." (Northern Telecom's self-imposed CFC-reduction goals exceed federal regulations; the company is moving to eliminate CFC solvent use by the end of 1991.)

As you encourage your employees to think green, they will begin to do a lot of your thinking for you. There are already thousands of North American examples of employee-inspired innovation, many of them very profitable. (We explore this important benefit of greening in Chapter Four.) Canadian Pacific Hotels & Resorts went to the front line; the company is asking their 10,000 employees for suggestions on how to green their

workplace. Environmental surveys have been distributed to each department.

Some companies are organizing permanent environmental committees, formal groups with representation from as many departments as possible. Each hotel in the Four Seasons Hotels & Resorts chain has a committee made up of volunteers who are fully committed to the company's recycling program and who take turns chairing the meetings. The committees' mandate—to initiate and administer recycling programs—has been vigorously carried out. In Seattle, for example, when the hotel ran into a problem with locating a market for its recyclables, committee members developed alliances with local businesses that helped revitalize the market for such goods.

Whether or not you initiate a green committee, your staff may decide to do so. Just before Earth Day 1990, a group of AT&T's New Jersey corridor employees, many of whose jobs have nothing to do with the environment, got together on their own initiative to form a group that calls itself "AT&T Employees in Action for the Environment." Their self-declared purpose is to "identify, communicate and effect actions that have a positive effect on the environment." This group of employees says that individuals can make a difference. "It's about personal accountability," says member Margaret Saidance. And this may be a key reason why such staff groupings can be so effective: they give people a sense they are doing something concrete and useful.

Another company that has discovered the usefulness of environmental committees is Ciba-Geigy, the Swiss chemical company, who told us that while environmentally sound chemistry begins in laboratories, it doesn't stop there. "Ciba-Geigy doesn't just have a corporate environmental policy," says Dr. Don Ridley, Canadian vice-president of health and safety, "we want everyone to get involved. Our staff have organized a committee of people with nonscientific backgrounds, and they report their ideas to us on a regular basis." This direct link with the senior executive suite is crucial to the success of environmental committees. However your company's green committee comes into being, make sure that it reports regularly to the green vice-president, and expect the vice-president to appear periodically at its meetings. Active senior management support helps guarantee that the committee will produce results.

Direct feedback on green recommendations and suggested innovations is important at all levels of the company's operation. As you develop in-house programs and encourage your staff to come up with green ideas, make sure that you communicate with them regularly and implement their suggestions. Staff will be encouraged to act further if they see that their ideas are actually being followed up by the company. In addition, use traditional means of communication, such as newsletters and meetings, to let your employees know where the company stands in the development and implementation of its green business strategy—new developments, success stories and other "good news" are particularly effective. And communication works to your advantage in another way: the more enthusiastic and up to date employees are, the more likely it is that they will be willing and able to get green projects up and running—fast.

If your employees genuinely believe you will act on their ideas they will respond, as the experience of the greenest companies already shows. In the late 1980s, the Monsanto Chemical Company decided to become "environmentally improved," so it announced to its employees that it wanted to reduce the emissions from its processes by 50 percent by the end of 1992. To accomplish this ambitious target, company executives turned to their staff and simply asked them, "How do you not make waste in the first place?" Monsanto knew that the people on the front lines understood their jobs best and believed that they could achieve this reduction goal by working with their staff. They were right. For example, the employees in one plant in Ireland designed a system for chemical by-product recycling that not only reduced the total amount of hazardous emissions, but also netted a 15 percent return on investment. Because of innovations like this, Monsanto was able to raise its reduction target from 50 percent to 90 percent, a commitment that soon became known as the "90 percent Pledge." Chairman Richard J. Mahoney says he has received more mail from staff on this initiative than on anything else the company has ever done.

One way of further converting your staff to environmental thinking is to include a green component in performance appraisals. This means that the compensation of a group or individual is partly determined by their environmental performance. In 1990 Conoco Inc., a Du Pont subsidiary, began an environmental bonus program. The program rewards individual employees who initiate environmental changes, and acknowledges individual plants that achieve environmental superiority. The company believes, says Jim Brigance, consultant, environmental communications, "that this program is really useful in spurring employee action. It's as much the public recognition of your efforts as the financial reward that makes the individual feel they're contributing to something worthwhile." Finally, don't restrict financial compensation or recognition to line staff: rewarding executives for performing well is also important. Ashland Oil gives hefty bonuses to managers who have demonstrated environmental initiative.

Hire Greener Managers

The greening of business has created a need for a new kind of manager. If you are serious about greening your company, you should hire graduates with a sure grasp of the new realities, people who are familiar with environmental issues and their impact on business.

"Recent stories in the *Wall Street Journal, New York Times, Chicago Tribune* and others have focused on the idea that business schools are the last of the professional schools to wake up to the importance of environmental matters," says Boston University professor James Post. "Law, public health and public administration courses have been doing it for years, but not business schools. Yet business clearly has the largest impact on the environment." However, companies across North America are now working with local business schools to correct this deficiency. For example, Boston University and the companies that work with the World Wildlife Fund's Corporate Conservation Council, including Du Pont Co., General Motors Corp. and Dow Chemical Co., recently invested US$200,000 in a pilot business-and-the-environment program. The seminar-style course is designed to take a careful look at the management implications of current environmental problems. Case studies help the students work through the implications of green issues on business planning, development, operations and cost accounting.

A similar program is now being offered by Canada's top business school, the University of Western Ontario. In 1989 a course called "Managing Sustainable Development" was launched with support from Dow Chemical Canada Inc. and Inco Limited. "The course," says Business Administration professor Richard Hodgson, "helps students come to grips with the complexities of sustainable development and to develop skills to formulate and implement policies that integrate economic progress with the quality of life and preservation of the biosphere."

Although business schools have been slow to respond to the demand for "green MBA" programs, the few courses offered have been extremely popular. Boston University, Western and other schools, such as Loyola University in New Orleans and the University of Minnesota, note record attendance at their green courses. Western's Hodgson says, "I've been teaching for twenty-five years and I can't think of a set of classes that's had a more enthusiastic response." But whether or not the courses are available, recent business graduates place concern for the environment at the top of the list of qualities they look for in a prospective employer. They want to work for a company with a good environmental report card. Evidence of this is offered by Jon Grant of Quaker Oats Canada. "We were interviewing candidates from Queen's University recently, and were surprised when the students asked us about our company's environmental record. I'm happy to say that we could respond in the affirmative." It seems the best candidates wanted to work for the greenest companies.

Being green is one way to ensure that you are the employer of choice when the labor market gets tight. This impression is corroborated by P.S. Dickey, manager, safety and environmental affairs, Shell Canada Limited, who flatly states: "In order to attract the best employees these days, you have to have strong environmental policies." In other words, the trend is not limited to hiring recent graduates. Headhunters confirm that awareness of green issues and practices is growing in importance for their clients—and among their most employable candidates.

Patrick received this message loud and clear when Loblaws Supermarkets ran an ad in the Toronto papers for a public relations manager. "We received twelve hundred applications," he recalls, "more than we'd ever received for any job before this. And what did most of the applicants cite as their reason for wanting to join Loblaws? Our environmental commitment—and a number of them were willing to take a pay cut to join the company. Even among our staff, I still get offers from people who want to work—on a volunteer basis, after hours—for the environmental department."

Not everyone, however, will be as keen about being green. It is inevitable that you will experience resistance from some people in your organization. The change in corporate culture is driven in part by a new and younger group, and age is often the demarcation line between those who will accept the change, and those who fight it. In addition, says Inco's vice-president Roy Aitken, middle managers are by nature the most conservative and resistant to change. "They're caught between upper management and the shop floor with their opposing agendas," he notes. "You have to be sophisticated when talking to the different levels within your own company."

Patrick says it's important to create the right balance. "Gradually, as the results of the environmental programs you managed to get approved roll in, even the skeptics will begin to see the benefits. After all, we were all in the dark ages about greening just a few short years ago."

Cooperate With Greener Unions

One of the benefits of the corporate greening process can be an improved relationship with your unionized employees. Although there is still often an adversarial relationship between management and labor, the environment may prove to be a common meeting ground. Unions are developing their own environmental agendas; make sure that you develop a comprehensive course of action that encourages a team spirit.

First, keep in mind the two most important elements of every labor agenda and how they relate to the environment:

1. *Jobs.* Unions realize that many of their members' jobs are in polluting industries and that the growing trend toward environmentally improved industrial practices will mean the closing of some factories and the loss of some jobs. If a mill is about to be shut down because of pollution, the natural union response is to fight to save its jobs.

2. *Health and Safety.* These related concerns have always been central for labor, and a union's negotiating position on environmental issues is generally approached from a health and safety point of view. This is likely to continue to be a key area.

Despite some standard posturing and some reactionary thinking, however, union members are increasingly motivated by the same concerns that are encouraging you to go green. They care about the well-being of the planet too. A sure sign that labor horizons are broadening is a recently published proposal of the International Confederation of Free Trade Unions (ICFTU). The ICFTU's policy paper on the environment—as approved by 87 million members in ninety-seven countries—makes many recommendations that could easily have come from a multinational corporation, including a ban on CFCs and an emphasis on developing alternative energy technologies. In North America, both the United Steelworkers of America and the Canadian Paperworkers' Union are working with Greenpeace to investigate environmental issues. Similar studies have been launched by other major unions. The goal of these initiatives is for trade unionists to become actively involved with the environmental issues that affect health and safety on the job and have a long-term impact on employment. They also want protection for workers who blow the whistle on companies that are breaking environmental laws.

To summarize, the differing objectives of management and labor won't disappear, but the growing interest in the environment represents a new opportunity for bridge building to organized labor. At the very least, it is crucial to make union workers full partners in corporate greening. "You can't control the environment from head office," says Inco's Roy Aitken. "You need to buy in at the front-line level, on the shop floor. There may be some resistance to new responsibilities which haven't been part of the employee's job description before. But persistence—and results—will win the day."

Recent experience suggests that Aitken is right. When a program to cut hazardous wastes was first suggested to shop floor workers at General Electric Co.'s aircraft-engines plant in Evendale, Ohio, they vetoed the idea. It simply looked like an additional responsibility they didn't need. However, a training program that reviewed the environmental advantages and potential cost reductions helped turn this early resistance into cooperation. As a result, waste at the plant has been reduced by 20 percent. General Electric is introducing similar programs at other plants, and some interesting new ideas generated from the shop floor—including fuel-efficient aircraft engines—are in the planning stages.

Green Management Is Better Management

As you begin to implement your green business strategy, you may see some changes that you did not anticipate. For one thing, by greening your company you will probably begin to alter the way you manage as well. The greenest organizations are often already the best-managed firms, with strong traditions of fair labor practices and a company-wide emphasis on quality. And companies that have been forced by circumstance to become more environmentally benign are becoming better managed in the process. Union Carbide, for example, frightened by the Bhopal tragedy and a subsequent takeover bid, made dramatic improvements in its management systems in a short period of time. Environmental policy was integral to this reform, which extended environmental awareness to all departments, not just to engineering or operations.

One component of this new management philosophy is increasing environmental accountability. Companies are creating explicit accountability systems for executives, shareholders and employees. Noranda Inc., for example, has a well-thought-out series of "minimum standards" to which its officers and directors must adhere. Here are two characteristic samples: "The Directors collectively would be responsible for carrying out diligent and thorough reviews of environmental reports provided by the Officers of the corporation" and "Review compliance with environmental legislation at reasonable intervals. Where there is non-compliance or potential non-compliance with environmental laws, others should ensure that all reasonable steps are taken to stop or prevent non-compliance." Each year Alcan Aluminum requires senior executives to decide what their environmental goals are and they are then held accountable for those targets. Today, companies that are going green are consulting with the staff of Monsanto, Noranda, Alcan and other leaders to assess their environmental management practices, and to emulate them. In sum, the green pioneers are demanding the highest possible standard of environmental awareness and management performance from their top people, and the companies that have been slower to move into greening are looking to the pioneers for guidance.

As the greening of your company gets underway, you will not only refine management skills but your managers will increasingly think differently. In the course of our interviews with senior executives of pioneering green businesses, we noted both a much more comprehensive approach to problem-solving than is traditional and an increased sense of responsibility toward employees. In the greenest organizations this is evident in a more mature treatment of union and non-union employees and an increased sense of the value of human assets.

One of the most important benefits of this new management philosophy is that morale will inevitably improve. Your employees will be aware that you are making decisions that affect more than the bottom line and they will recognize that they are doing something to help solve the environmental problems we all face. It is not news that good morale is good for productivity, but some companies have been slow to remember this rule when it comes to the environment. In the 1970s, when a bunker mentality ruled in the chemical industry, companies found it difficult to keep staff, and morale plummeted. Many chemical multi-nationals have turned this around by championing environmental innovations. Today, the greenest companies—chemical manufacturers and others—have staff who will go the extra mile to reach their environmental goals. "Our employees want to work for a clean and green company," says Alcan's Dr. Raymond Brouzes. "They want to make a difference at work, as well as at home."

▫ FOUR ▫

Clean Up Your Own Act

As your staff becomes committed to an environmental way of thinking they will generate all sorts of innovative ideas for cleaner operating methods and greener products. Already, you may have acted on some of these. To be thorough, however, cleaning up your company's act must be approached in a systematic way, the same way it approaches any other issue of strategic importance. Otherwise, at the press conference announcing the launch of your new line of green products an environmentalist is sure to raise some embarrassing questions for your president. "That incident last week in your Chicago warehouse, the one where the transformer leaked PCBs. Has that spill been cleaned up yet?" "And what about your plant in Texas that's having a fight with the local community about emissions standards? Are they still threatening a class action suit for the health problems they claim your plant has caused?" Or perhaps you may go public with the environmental improvements in one division, while another is being charged with releasing toxic effluent. As many companies have discovered, there's much more to greening than simply sticking a label on a product and calling it environmentally friendly.

There are many good reasons for cleaning up your company, not least of which is that it is the right thing to do. Overall, however, the reasons reduce to this simple truth: it's good for business. It will put your company and what it sells in the vanguard of a revolution, and it may mean the difference between increasing your sales and staring at a shrinking market share. Rather than waiting for and reacting to changes in the marketplace, you will be one of the leaders that other companies will struggle to emulate. The organizations with the greenest images will attract the best employees and the most new investment, and they will be favored when the government is looking to encourage exports or regional economic development. In addition to these long-term rewards, there are a number of short-term benefits to be gained by launching a systematic clean-up review:

- You will identify crises that are waiting to happen, which means that you won't have to embark on a hasty and costly clean-up or pay a stiff fine after an embarrassing visit from a government inspector.
- You will almost certainly save money.
- Your staff will come up with all sorts of ideas for innovations that will make your operations more efficient and your products more appealing to green consumers.
- You will identify new business opportunities.
- You will identify areas of potential liability and find techniques for lowering your insurance premiums and reducing your company's level of environmental risk.

Businesses that don't take this process seriously and attempt to do the minimum they can get away with will pay a higher price in fines or lost market share. Superficial greening is not only unpopular with regulators, it is anathema to environmental groups and will increasingly backfire with consumers. A thorough greening of every aspect of your operation simply makes good business sense in the 1990s. Analyze your company from top to bottom and inside out in search of environmental problems and opportunities.

The Environmental Audit

Both financially and socially, the most rewarding payback for your company is to undertake an environmental audit. If you invest in such an audit, you will not be alone. In the United States, environmental auditors will bill businesses an estimated US$1 billion in 1991. In other words, even if you are not hiring these green experts, your competitors are.

Not every green pioneer conducts a thorough audit before making any public moves. As we have already pointed out, Loblaws was a case in point. During the process of developing the company's first environmentally friendly products it realized the importance of complete corporate greening. Recently Loblaw Companies Limited hired Canada's largest management consulting firm, Ernst & Young, to conduct a comprehensive audit of all its operations. It was in part the learning experience involved in bringing those first green products to market that convinced the company just how important an audit was. In an ideal world, you would always conduct your audit first, to make sure that no toxic skeletons in your closet would come to light on the day of your product launch. But in the real world, this won't always be the case. The main point is to undertake an audit as soon as possible, no matter how cursory it is in its initial stages.

An environmental audit is a systematic, thorough review of the operations and practices of a business to identify environmental problems—or potential problems—and recommend what to do about them. It will also tell you what you are already doing well. Often audits spot obvious ways of both cleaning up and saving money. They are conducted by environmental consulting firms, or by any one of a number of other companies that offer environmental consulting services, such as accounting-management consulting firms, engineering organizations, waste management companies and legal firms.

The term environmental audit covers a range of different activities, all of which come under the general heading of environmental analysis. Unlike a financial audit, an environmental audit is not yet a standardized procedure with recognized rules. The type of audit you order for your company will depend on your objectives. Here are some possibilities:

- a review of performance against regulations, conducted mainly for management
- an environmental impact assessment of proposed development, such as a building or hydroelectric dam, conducted as part of a governmental environmental review process
- environmental risk assessment, carried out as part of the purchase or sale of a business
- independent professional opinion on an organization's environmental management systems based on specific environmental management principles

As the environmental audit industry is still evolving, there are as yet no standards in place, but this situation will change soon. "We need established guidelines on what an audit should comprise," says John Elkington, president of SustainAbility, a U.K. environmental consulting firm. "As environmental pressures increase, there is going to be a problem of insufficient accredited auditors. It's an area where business is going to have to wake up very quickly." Associations for auditing professionals are being established across North America and Western Europe. Task forces composed of environmental consultants, business people, regulators and chartered accountants (whose expertise in financial audits provides a useful perspective) are working to establish environmental auditing standards. But until these standards are in place, companies must be extremely careful in choosing an auditor.

The most common sort of "environmental audit" conducted for management is a periodic review of performance against regulations. The review of performance we deem most valuable is a comprehensive review, like the one defined by the International Chamber of Commerce as "a management tool comprising a systematic, documented, periodic and objective evaluation of how well environmental organization, management and equipment are performing, with the aim of helping to safeguard the environment." This type of audit will be discussed in the pages that follow.

Your company's audit has two separate though related goals. The first is defensive, to ensure that your operations are in compliance with government regulations and company standards. The second is offensive, to determine the effectiveness of operations and controls already in place, assess your current level of environmental risk and identify new areas where improvements could be made. For example, because regulations are changing so fast, an audit may reveal that your company's waste management practices border on illegality. A lawyer we know recently said that often the green ink on a regulation has not quite dried when it is superceded by a new regulation. But legal or not, it often turns out that, with minor changes in procedure, significant cost reductions can be achieved and embarrassing publicity avoided.

Many resource-sector companies and other large firms are already undertaking regular, comprehensive audits. U.S. chemical and oil giants were among the first to use these as a green management tool, primarily as a way to ensure that they remained in compliance with the growing list of government regulations that governed their operations in the 1970s and 1980s. Arthur D. Little Inc. (ADL), a leading North American consulting and environmental management firm, estimates that in the early 1980s chemical and petrochemical clients accounted for 80 percent of its business. Gradually, however, auditing is becoming more commonplace in lower-risk industry sectors such as manufacturing, high-tech, food processing and as other small- and medium-sized businesses discover the advantages of a thorough environmental self-analysis.

A typical environmental audit includes seven basic steps. Use these steps as guidelines only; the procedure you follow will depend on your objectives and your auditor's approach.

1. Establish the Audit's Objectives

Before you do anything else, determine in a broad way what you want the audit to accomplish. It can be cursory or comprehensive, but again, we recommend the latter. A broad-ranging audit will identify crisis areas and allow you to map out a strategy for greening each area according to a schedule that works for your company. The following are some of the audit objectives noted by executives and auditors:

- to verify compliance with government regulations
- to highlight and correct hazardous practices or to identify potentially hazardous sites
- to measure your company against your industry's code of operating principles
- to review and assess the environmental policies and procedures that are in place, or to develop new practices and standards in accordance with changing regulations
- to identify areas for increasing raw material or resource efficiencies
- to identify waste management opportunities, to reduce or eliminate by-products
- to develop an internal auditing program that can be carried out on an annual basis
- to identify new business opportunities
- to identify areas where green initiatives can be introduced
- to review and update personnel training and development policies
- to identify where new staff are required or where current requirements can be reduced
- to adjust operating and capital budgets accordingly

An effective auditor should accomplish all of these things and then produce a written plan of action that is practical and cost-effective. Whether you decide to do a simple study with basic strategy recommendations or to make detailed environmental auditing an integral part of your company's ongoing strategic planning, an audit makes sense. "The true costs of the Chernobyl accident may reach $430 billion by the year 2000," Patrick comments. "The reasons for auditing could not be clearer than this incredible figure and the horrendous effect the accident had on local communities."

2. Select an Auditor

In general, most companies hire an outside firm for their first audit because the auditor's expertise and objectivity are useful in helping staff become accustomed to viewing their organization through a green filter. Some enterprises, however, develop an internal audit team. This route was taken by Noranda Inc., a resource-sector company with holdings in forestry, minerals, manufacturing and energy. One of the benefits of an internal audit team, according to Dr. Frank Frantisak, Noranda Inc.'s vice-president of environmental services, was the exposure of audit team members to outstanding management systems in place at a number of Noranda's plants: often the exchange of operating practices between different divisions of the company resulted in some immediate, and relatively painless, improvements. The auditing team consists of fifty-five Noranda employees, each of whom devotes part of his or her time to auditing, and the rest to regular job responsibilities in chemistry, engineering, environmental science, medicine and emergency-response. Arthur D. Little Inc. helped Noranda set up its program, but the company now runs it independently. Third-party external auditors are used only for divestiture reviews (prior to selling one of its operations), where an unbiased assessment of potential liabilities and costs is of special importance.

Union Carbide has taken a different approach, opting for a combination of internal and external expertise, which is what we generally recommend. Its worldwide corporate environmental program includes eighteen full-time auditors, among them a number of retired Union Carbide managers. This group was trained by consultants from Arthur D. Little Inc. who were called in to help Union Carbide develop its internal audit program in the days that followed the Bhopal incident. In particularly sensitive areas, the entire audit team is comprised of ADL staff. The "sensitive work" category includes activities such as examining an operating unit inside a particular plant to determine its potential for "episodic catastrophic release."

If you decide to hire an outside auditor, the one you choose will depend on what you want to accomplish. Some companies prefer to call in experts to deal with specific areas of operations, for instance to examine their waste disposal or energy consumption practices. However, depending on the nature of your business, your management philosophy and the size of your company it may be wise to carry out a cursory review internally to help determine auditing requirements.

If you cannot afford an auditor's fees, which range from as little as US$500 to audit a restaurant or small retail outlet to hundreds of thousands for a detailed top-to-bottom analysis of a large company, you will be able to hire a consultant who will provide your staff with training seminars designed to teach auditing skills. There are also books on the market that enumerate the fundamentals and techniques of environmental auditing in great detail. But these approaches are recommended only if you have staff that are already technically competent in the field of environmental protection. While a self-administered audit is better than no audit at all, the stakes make it worth investing in the best audit you can afford. With self-auditing you may not see the forest for the trees.

Choose an auditor who has been recommended by another company in your industry or by a respected colleague. "When

I'm making speeches about Loblaws' successful G.R.E.E.N line and updating companies on how we approached the greening of our organization, executives often ask me how to select an auditor," Patrick comments. "I advise them to choose a firm that has been recommended by a company that suffered a serious environmental incident, and with the assistance of their auditor, was able to establish new standards. Alternately, choose an auditor who has been recommended by a company with environmental management systems that are held in high esteem by regulators, environmentalists and the community."

Finally, environmental reviews are normally conducted by a team of professionals, rather than one consultant. The team approach is necessary because of the sheer breadth of the investigation that needs to be done and also because a wide range of experience and knowledge is required to produce a comprehensive review. Depending on the assignment, the expertise of team members should include the following:

- depending on the materials being handled, specific knowledge of their environmental impact
- knowledge of environmental regulations applicable to the industry
- knowledge of environmental auditing skills and techniques, and a systematic approach to conducting an audit
- knowledge of environmental protection strategies, including management systems, operating practices and emergency-response policies
- a basic technical understanding of the type of operation and equipment being audited

3. Set the Stage for the Audit

First, establish a steering committee or appoint a senior executive who will ensure that your company's objectives are covered by the audit. All audit communication will flow through this liaison person or group.

Then take measures to ensure staff support of the audit. This is one of the most important conditions of a successful audit process. The very word "audit" may strike fear into the hearts of staff and management, many of whom have bad memories of intrusive financial audits. Early on, convey the message that an environmental audit is not a witch hunt, but is intended to make your company as environmentally sound as possible, at a pace that is feasible, taking day-to-day operations into account. Special thought must be given to advising union personnel about the audit—you will obviously need their cooperation if all objectives are to be accomplished. Let all employees know that you need their support in order to ensure the audit's success.

If you have already taken concrete steps to bring your team on side and your employees are starting to think green, staff support will come much more easily, of course. But whether or not this kind of preparation has been done, the environmental audit steering committee should work with your human resources department to prepare employees for the audit process. This can be done by advising them through staff publications, with their pay cheques or at special meetings. Loblaws set the stage for its environmental audit by giving each of its senior executives and key middle managers a copy of Warner Troyer's *Preserving Our World*. Dow Canada's approach was to hold an "environmental awareness day": it invited a pollster, a government regulator, an environmental consultant and a green businessman to take part in a panel discussion at a special seminar for senior managers.

Next, select a site for a test audit. Most large companies undertake a small-scale audit like this first, before involving all of their operations. If possible, choose a location that is environmentally sensitive or includes a number of potential hazards, so that your test will include as many variables as possible. Loblaws, for example, chose a warehouse in a Toronto suburb as a location to conduct a small-scale audit. Contact the facility that is to be audited, advise its management and obtain any necessary preliminary information. Determine the test audit's final objectives, priorities and any requirements necessary for the procedure.

Set the date for the audit, and advise your staff and the consultant or audit team. Have the steering committee or a senior executive brief the environmental audit consultant about your objectives and the scope of the audit, so that your auditor can begin to develop the protocols (or audit procedures) to be used.

4. Conduct the Audit

The consultant or audit team will conduct the environmental audit over a period of weeks, or perhaps months, depending on its complexity and the size of your operation. Each audit will include a number of distinct steps, along these lines:

- an opening meeting to review objectives
- a review of existing documentation, such as policies, procedures and appropriate legislation
- an orientation tour of the facility
- the gathering of information, including: interviewing and observing staff; testing and observing equipment; checking locations of safety and hazard warning signage; reviewing copies of discharge permits and records of actual discharge levels; observing actual operating procedures and staff training; observing operability, maintenance and appropriateness of pollution-control equipment; where appropriate, staging of a mock incident to assess emergency preparedness and crisis management strategies

Sometimes at the outset an audit will uncover a serious environmental problem. If so, don't wait until the entire audit process is complete to take remedial action. Start working on the problem immediately while the audit continues.

5. Analyze the Audit Information

When the audit team has completed its investigation, it will begin a detailed analysis of the data it has gathered. To aid this process, most auditors follow a set of procedures they have prepared before starting the audit, which allow them to immediately identify problems and opportunities for improvements. The chart on page 82 shows a typical diagnostic framework, with relevant information slotted in.

You can quickly see from this example that such a diagnosis leads automatically to possible prescriptions. By simply comparing your company's actual practice (the final column) with the current best practice in the industry (the second-last column), options for action become obvious. However, what the auditor actually recommends in the final report will depend on the audit's terms of reference and how urgent or expensive the improvements are.

Once all the information has been analyzed along these lines, taking into account the company's particular circumstances, the auditor will meet with the liaison person or group to discuss the findings and to take note of any new developments, such as regulations that have been passed since the audit began or new employee health and safety policies. The auditor will then write a final report and present it to management and the board of directors.

6. The Final Report

Although the nature of the auditor's final report will depend on what you've asked for and what you are paying for, in our opinion it should contain the following elements:

- A detailed assessment of the *environmental problems* in your entire operation, including your administrative offices, and recommendations as to how to fix these problems. A good audit will also spotlight opportunities to save money while cleaning up your operations.
- A detailed assessment of your *current management structure* and how it can most effectively implement the audit's recommendations. The report should include some specific recommendations indicating where your management practices can be improved to make environmental issues more of a priority.

Source of Potential Environmental Impact	Potential Environmental Impact	Regulations Exist	Name of Regulations	Written Corporate Practice Procedures	Best Industry Practice	Actual Practice/ Procedure
decommissioned transformers and/or capacitors containing PCBs	major risk in the event of a fire	yes	(name of provincial/ state and federal regulations) including Environmental Protection Act	none	Store in an approved, fire proof, secure area; secondary containment; alarm system	Transformers exposed
underground fuel tanks	contamination of groundwater due to leakage	yes	(name of provincial/ state and federal regulations)	none	Replace tanks with above-ground, or double-walled, with leak detectors	Existing underground tanks single-hulled; new tanks follow best industry practices
chlorofluorocarbon used in air conditioning	ozone depletion	yes	(name of provincial/ state and federal regulations) including federal compliance with Montral Protocol	none	CFCs collected for recycling; replace system with new technology	New system in capital budget for 1992-93
asbestos insulation	suspected carcinogen	yes	(name of provincial/ state and federal regulations)	Reduce exposure where possible	Conduct surveys to identify presence of asbestos; remove any that poses risk	Asbestos in old wing only; not exposed
pesticide use	bioaccumulation in surrounding property; contamination of local stream; disposal of excess product and packaging	yes	(name of provincial/ state and federal regulations) such as Pesticide Control Act	none	Review range of pesticides available; train staff in use and disposal	Maintenance staff responsibility

- A detailed *action plan*, recommending what to do in what order, how fast and at what cost, and outlining what benefits can be expected.

In sum, the audit's objective is to provide a performance review, with the goal of bringing your operation up to existing environmental standards. The audit's audience is management: we recommend that you distribute the report to key people within your organization, to help them understand the challenges, and to show you are committed to cleaning up the company. Noranda, for instance, gives background details and copies of the final audit report and action plan to all of its plant managers.

7. Follow Up on Your Audit

How you deal with the mass of information that has now landed on your desk will tell a great deal about how genuinely you are committed to going green. Of course, your plans of action will depend on the seriousness of the problems detected and how much money you have allocated in the budget. In general, however, it is important to view the audit findings as strategic opportunities, not as mere brush fires to be put out. Here is Tony Leighton, the publisher of *EcoSource*, a newsletter that looks at environmental issues in a business framework and carries reports of international green business ventures: "The report that emerges from the audit works as a road map for senior executives who want to find their way through the environmental morass, and a how-to manual for employees who want to help, but don't know where to start."

Whatever else you do, move quickly to implement the environmental action plan you decide on. Establish a timetable with target dates for each phase of your internal clean-up and establish review dates when overall progress will be checked. Devise a monitoring program to ensure compliance on an ongoing basis, and assign responsibility and authority to specific employees. Set up an environmental record-keeping system (the audit's findings will be the first entry in this ongoing documentation of each facility's environmental practices) and make sure that your next operating and capital budgets include an environmental component that will cover the cost of new procedures, new or revamped equipment, and the hiring or retraining of personnel. Even before the ink is dry on the auditor's report, schedule your next audit to take place one year later. (If the first was a test audit, this will also be the time to commission an audit of your entire company.)

For most companies operating in North America today, an annual environmental audit will become standard practice, though in the past, even companies that undertook regular audits have done so as infrequently as every four years. Given the pace of change, annual audits are now a good idea even for organizations that are not involved in high-risk enterprises such as chemical production. Apart from the other benefits of annual audits, you will be able to seize opportunities more quickly. In fact, it is often useful to monitor your environmental progress even more closely. Some consultants recommend a new audit whenever there are changes in regulations, technology, disposal practices or the price of raw materials. (However, this type of audit, called a reactive audit, is limited to a specific area of concern, as opposed to the more comprehensive, regularly scheduled audit.)

As a general rule, the results of environmental audits are confidential and are for the company's internal use only. But disclosure of results is a hotly contested issue. Many legal firms advise companies to hire a lawyer, who will in turn hire the auditor, so that all reports remain under solicitor-client confidentiality rules. But some environmental law practitioners say that this protection may be successfully challenged in the courts. Noranda's Dr. Frank Frantisak says that, "the question of report accessibility by government agencies and by court-directed disclosure is one that industry and legislators are struggling with.

Noranda has concluded that the benefits flowing from the auditing program far outweigh any negative concerns associated with disclosure." It is up to you to decide whether or not to reveal the results of your audit, but we recommend that as quickly as possible, you find a way to do so. While such openness is still unusual, it will be in your long-term best interest to make it a practice to be as open as possible with the local community and with regulators.

Your audit is a snapshot that tells you how green your organization is at a particular moment in time. As such, it has great value as a tool for beginning the clean-up process. Patrick cautions companies not to view an audit as "a way to cover up bad practices. This kind of thinking is a waste of money, shows an alarming ignorance of the real costs of liability and will ultimately saddle your company with a loss of credibility with government and the public, and may even result in whistle blowing by staff."

We suggest that you regard the environmental audit process as an important—and inevitable—cost of doing business in North America today, as essential as the benefit package for your employees. Even if an audit isn't mandatory at the moment, it will be in the near future. Business analysts predict that in the next two years the European Community will require companies to carry out regular environmental audits. National governments may get there even sooner: the British Labour Party is backing legislation that would make audits mandatory for all companies operating within Britain's borders. It won't be long before this trend reaches this side of the Atlantic as well. Regulators are introducing disclosure measures such as the U.S. Toxic Release Inventory, so it is clearly in your best interest to establish an audit history now, as an indication that your company is taking important steps toward cleaning up.

But whether or not governments in North America move quickly to require audits—and it is likely that they will—a combination of other forces is making them unavoidable. One of the most important of these is the spillover effect as more and more companies, especially some of the continent's largest enterprises, voluntarily conduct regular and rigorous audits themselves. As these firms clean up their acts, they will require their suppliers to do the same, and this will have a domino effect on all businesses that do business with these cleaner companies. Meanwhile, insurers will continue to demand that you lower your level of environmental risk, investors will want to see environmental report cards before they hand you their money and ordinary consumers will increasingly differentiate between truly green companies and those where green is only skin deep. In short, this decade will likely see environmental audits become standard operating procedure for North American companies outside the resource sector, where they have long been standard practice.

Getting Your Clean-Up Underway

The auditor's report and recommendations comprise a kind of "greenprint" for cleaning up your company, but they are only part of the information at your disposal. Auditors aren't perfect, and they aren't as close to your operations as your own employees. In a fully green corporate culture, small, everyday environmental audits are taking place in every corner of the company: a truck driver notices that if he loads his truck a different way he can get more into a load, thereby reducing frequency of trips and the quantity of fuel required; an office worker reports that while the recycling program you've set up works fine for paper, it is doing much more poorly on plastic; your comptroller begins to track environmental measures within your company and discovers that there are some significant money-saving opportunities. The contributions of your staff are invaluable additions to your own expertise and that of your environmental consultants.

As you move to clean up your company from executive suite to shop floor, draw on all your information resources: your own employees, environmental groups and consultants, government departments, local community groups and chambers of commerce, trade or business associations and all your contacts at other companies. Although you will have to establish your own parameters for information gathering and action, the following pages will sketch out the possible scope of your company's clean-up process.

In order to do this, we have arbitrarily divided your operations into four categories: the office, the plant, the neighborhood and your industry. The *office* includes all your white-collar operations. The *plant* comprises everything from your warehouse to your factory, mine or lumbering operation. The *neighborhood* is the local community in which each of your enterprises is located. Your *industry* includes others who are in the same business or who use many of the same raw materials in their processes. These four categories occasionally overlap, but for the most part they present distinct challenges and opportunities for turning your company green.

The Office

Even before you conducted your audit, you may well have started the greening of your office, perhaps as part of bringing your team on side. Office workers generally come from the segment of society that is most concerned about the environment and are already doing things like recycling in their own homes. As a result they are often very enthusiastic when their company brings similar measures into the workplace. In fact, office greening has become such a fast-growing phenomenon that books are being dedicated to the subject. One of the most recent is *The Green Office Manual* by Noel Desautels of Environmental Resources, a Toronto-based environmental consulting firm. As Desautels points out, office practices can be modified without a huge investment and with very few changes in day-to-day procedures.

For simplicity, we've subdivided office clean-up into six

sections: Reduce, Reuse, Recycle, Save Energy, Improve the Interior Environment and Adopt Greener Purchasing Policies. The advice and examples that follow should give you a good idea of what you can do quickly and cost-effectively to clean up the office.

A major theme of this and the subsequent section, on cleaning up the plant, is the money you can save by sending less garbage to the landfill. Throughout North America, rising landfill costs mean that almost everything you throw away is costing more. In Metropolitan Toronto dumping charges have gone from CDN$18 to $110 per ton in only two years, and this sort of trend is typical of major urban areas across the continent. In Europe, where population is denser and land more scarce, tipping charges are now as much as ten times higher than those of the early 1980s.

Reduce

"Reduce" is the first commandment of environmental management. By eliminating what you don't need, you can lower your costs, both at the front end, when you buy supplies, and at the back end, when you send fewer truckloads of garbage off to the local landfill. Here are some good ideas that the companies we interviewed have already tried successfully:

1. Use both sides of all paper (and when you order your new photocopier, make sure it is a duplexor).
2. Invest in low-flush toilets (or install water dams in existing tanks) and water-efficient faucets and showerheads.
3. Use less packaging, modify procedures to require fewer hard copies of an invoice or packing slip.
4. Make sure your company cars have regular maintenance checks to ensure that they are fuel efficient.
5. Use a phone instead of sending a memo, and use electronic media wherever possible (teleconferencing, for example).
6. Arrange car pooling, walking, biking and public transit options for staff.

Reuse

"Reuse" means make something do its job over and over again, such as putting reusable dishes in the lunchroom or cafeteria, or designing a company mug to encourage staff to switch from disposable coffee cups. Use refillable containers wherever possible—printer cartridges (some suppliers will take back your empty cartridges), pens, boxes and envelopes that can be used repeatedly, rather than discarded after one use. Exchange surplus office furnishings and equipment between departments and divisions—or hold an annual furniture exchange so staff can take your company discards home. Some companies contact local charities and donate used furniture to families in need. Some companies have even set a target date to eliminate disposables from the office altogether.

Recycle

Recycling programs are sometimes referred to by business as "trash for cash." They are relatively easy to introduce and can have an immediate and positive impact on the balance sheet. In November 1989, the Toronto-Dominion Centre, Canada's largest office complex, with four towers and more than two hundred offices, launched a massive paper recycling program. Building staff prepared for a year before the program got underway, starting with an initial feasibility study. Before the plan was implemented, tenants had to be trained to separate various types of recyclable paper and carboard at their desks. By start-up date, every desk had two separate waste containers listing acceptable materials. Cleaning staff were responsible for collection and for dropping off the material collected at the loading docks for sorting. During its first week of operation, the program recycled twelve tons of corrugated cardboard and paper. "We spent CDN$30,000 just for the equipment we needed to get started," says Bill Merks, manager of housekeeping, "and Browning and Ferris Industries, who operate the recycling program for us, spent an additional $100,000." But with landfill space becoming increasingly difficult to obtain, and regulations regarding what can be dumped also becoming much more strict, the program actually turned a profit. The operation recycles twenty-five tons of paper and cardboard each week, with cardboard selling for $20 a ton and up, and computer paper netting as much as $200 a ton. Glass is next on the recycling agenda; six tenants are currently involved in a trial program. Only a year after developing a similar program, New York City's World Trade Center now recycles 22.5 tons of paper *each day*. And a June 1990 poll by the International Facility Management Association found that 77 percent of its members have an office recycling program.

The American Paper Institute estimates that 40 percent of all paper produced in 1995 will be recycled, whereas only 20 percent is recycled today. Clearly, the recycled fiber for this paper will have to come primarily from our offices and factories, where the majority of paper waste is created. Some pulp and paper industry insiders refer to this new source of raw materials as "the urban forest."

Save Energy

There are a multitude of ways to reduce your office energy consumption, and usually saving money in the process. In many areas local area utilities have programs that underwrite conservation measures. By reducing demand, a utility can postpone the need to invest in new capacity, and some two hundred utilities across the continent are already working on energy-efficiency programs. These programs provide support that ranges from a free energy audit to substantial cash subsidies for energy-saving retrofits of lightbulbs, appliances and equipment. Your local utility may also subsidize your purchase of new, more efficient water heaters, revamped cooling systems or the cost of pipe insulation.

If the utility you deal with has not yet started such an energy-conservation program, there are resources you can call upon for assistance, including energy consultants. One of the best known of these, the Rocky Mountain Institute, helped Compaq Computer design a new lighting program for its offices. The improvements cut Compaq's lighting bill in half and reduced its overall electrical charges by 21 percent: the cost of lighting a one-million-square-foot area went from US$1.21 per square foot to 96 cents, for a saving of $250,000 annually.

While your environmental audit may have identified areas where such improvements can be made, it is not a true energy audit. An energy audit has to be performed by specialists—either from your local utility or from energy management firms. For example, many companies that sell energy control systems for buildings also have experts who conduct energy audits. These firms will audit your facilities and prescribe changes that can reduce your energy bill significantly.

Improve the Interior Environment
The World Health Organization estimates that 30 percent of all office buildings are unhealthy, primarily because of high levels of carbon dioxide in the air; the U.S. Environmental Protection Agency estimates that indoor air pollution is costing American industry US$1 billion a year in lost office time and medical costs. The source of the bad air can be as simple as cigarette smoke, or as hard to detect as radon gas, PCBs, emissions from synthetic carpeting or laser printer ink, or inefficient (and often dirty) air filtration systems.

Developers such as The Cadillac Fairview Corporation are extremely concerned about the "sick building syndrome." All new buildings are being designed to provide cleaner air and a healthier working environment. Meanwhile, older buildings, including shopping centers, are being retrofitted with new air filtration equipment, helping to eliminate part of the problem.

No North American company has yet gone as far as the extraordinary new headquarters of NMB Bank in Amsterdam, which incorporates a long list of "humanistically balanced" and "environmentally sound" design elements. The building's exterior design deflects traffic noise and reduces the impact of the wind. A brightly lit interior atrium, filled with plants and trees, breathes oxygen into the air, and stairs are used for most movement between floors, restricting elevators to long-distance climbs. Windows are placed so as to collect light, which is dispersed by reflective materials through the central atrium, which in turn reflects it back into windowless office areas. The project won a design award, and uses 40 percent less energy than a comparable buildings where environmental factors have not been taken into account. But the biggest bonus has been a 25 percent drop in absenteeism among employees who moved from the company's other offices.

Adopt Greener Purchasing Policies

Greener purchasing policies—for both the office and the plant— have a ripple effect: they create a demand for greener products, that forces your suppliers to follow your example. In one vivid example the Government of Canada's recently implemented green purchasing policy has put pressure on suppliers to go green. The policy is worth CDN$9 billion per year for companies who are producing greener goods and services.

The more you know about environmental issues, the more rigorous your purchasing policy can become. However, some general rules apply to all companies setting up new policies. Where possible, buy recyclable products and products made from recycled materials. Buy in bulk (no more "single serving size" coffee creamers). Tell your suppliers you want them to reduce excess materials and packaging where possible. Use products with non-toxic ingredients (paints, cleaning solutions). Consider using alternative fuels or more environmentally friendly gasoline, such as lead-free.

The Body Shop, one of the most successful health and beauty product companies in the world, with sales in the range of US$500 million, is well known for its ethical purchasing policies.

The company has a comprehensive list of principles that its suppliers are expected to adhere to. For example, it buys cosmetic products and ingredients only from companies that do not test on animals, and it screens its suppliers' operations at six-month intervals to ensure that they are following this rule.

Another company that has generated a lot of good press for its environmentally responsible practices is the Vermont-based ice cream company, Ben & Jerry's Homemade, Inc. When the company wanted to begin purchasing recycled paper for its offices, it was put off by the 40 percent premium charged for recycled stock. In response, it organized a consortium of local firms that purchases recycled materials in bulk, allowing the company to buy recycled goods at a cost that is comparable to that of non-recycled.

Greener purchasing policies can have a positive effect on the marketplace—by creating a demand for recycled products and by encouraging suppliers to follow suit. Roots, a major Canadian clothing manufacturer and retailer, now requires its suppliers to carry out regular environmental assessments of their operations and to submit the results of these reviews. Finally, buying greener goods may be an area where companies that do not have the management base or financial freedom to make a large environmental commitment at this stage can make their concerns felt.

Cleaning up the office is one of the most common ways companies begin the greening process. Typically these measures are enthusiastically supported by staff, raising morale even when they don't save a lot of money.

The Plant

While office greening can be rewarding and implemented quickly, it takes time to green the "plant," a term we are using to include facilities ranging from a warehouse to a mining operation. Many of the changes you'll be making will take time—Dow Chemical Switzerland took five years to get its waste-minimization policy underway—but they are vital. While the main theme of cleaning up the office may have been to reduce waste, the overall focus of plant greening is the elimination of pollution in all its forms. This is chiefly accomplished by preventing pollution at source—in products and manufacturing processes—rather than reducing it after it has been created. While this idea is far from new, it is not yet widely accepted.

The potential dividends in cleaning up the plant are many times greater than those generated by cleaning up the office. Kodak's Chairman Kay Whitmore knew the benefits and recently charged his staff with the following: "In all of your strategic and business planning, you will look at the product through its full life cycle: manufacturing, processing, waste, retailing, marketing and disposal." The investment may be major, but the payback for cleaning up your factory, refinery or sawmill can be substantial. One of the reasons is that the cost of disposing of hazardous solid waste is rising even faster than the cost of getting rid of conventional solid waste. In the United States, hazardous waste disposal costs jumped from about US$80 a tonne in the early 1980s to $225 today. In Europe, they are ten times higher than a decade ago. And as community opposition to such disposal sites increases, costs will escalate further.

The primary opposition to environmental regulations has long been the belief that effective corporate initiatives to reduce pollution, such as new equipment or waste treatment plants, would require hefty capital investments and entail increased operating costs. However, when some of these companies (and their industry associations) conducted cost/benefit analyses, they were surprised to discover that cleaner, greener operations could actually save them money.

The firms profiled in this section experienced specific environmental and financial benefits from their clean-up efforts. For example, 3M's Pollution Prevention Pays program (3P) has cut in half the amount of pollution the company generates per unit of production, and it has resulted in a saving of US$500 million since 1975. The company recognized early on that it is more environmentally effective, technically sound and less costly to operate in this new way, and that by documenting the program's results, it could justify similar moves in the future. It defines four distinct payoffs for projects under the 3P banner:

1. Eliminate or reduce a pollutant.
2. Benefit the environment additionally through reduced energy use or more efficient use of materials and resources.
3. Demonstrate technical innovation.
4. Save money through the avoidance or deferral of pollution-control equipment costs, reduced operating and material expenses or increased sales of an existing or new products.

According to 3M, these payoffs are achieved by focusing on four categories: Recover Resources, Modify Processes, Redesign Equipment, and Reformulate. The fifth is Save Energy. Although often an integral part of the first four, saving energy is important enough to be discussed separately. "Any company that isn't capitalizing on these new ideas," Patrick believes, "is near-sighted—they're going to be left behind very quickly. As their competitors intensify efforts to reduce emissions, the demand for their 'dirty' products will diminish rapidly—no-one will be able to afford them."

Recover Resources

The single most promising green idea may be this one: that what used to be seen as *waste* is now regarded as a potential *resource*. In these terms, a resource is any substance that you can recover and either reuse yourself or sell to someone else. It is waste with a dollar value. Industrial resource recovery extends along a broad spectrum, from recycling solid materials such as corrugated cardboard to capturing and reusing by-products of an industrial process such as oil refining. For example, Du Pont produces 3,600 tonnes of a toxic chemical (hexamethyleneimine) each year as a by-product of manufacturing nylon. It used to have to dispose of this chemical in hazardous waste dumps. Today, the company has a market for the product in the pharmaceutical industry, and demand exceeds supply. Union Carbide also recycles or reuses 50 percent of its hazardous solid wastes, which were once a huge disposal headache. In the first six months of 1989, the company recycled, reclaimed or sold 82 million pounds of this waste, generating US$3.5 million in revenue and avoiding US$8.5 million in disposal costs.

There are other immediate benefits to resource recovery than the financial payoff; it is an important element in the development of sustainable practices. And in the long run, as the cost of resources escalates throughout the 1990s, resource recovery will become an essential part of doing business.

Modify Processes

Process modification means altering something you do so that you can achieve one of the following results:

- reduce potential risk
- decrease negative environmental impact (or actively make its net effect environmentally benign)
- use less energy.

Here are four examples from three different industries that illustrate this important idea. AT&T, as one of the world's largest users of chlorofluorocarbons (CFCs) which contribute to ozone depletion, has been investing in research and development of an alternative agent to clean its circuit boards. (One of the CFC alternatives discovered was plain soap and water.) Rather than stopping there, however, the company asked itself whether it could eliminate the need to clean circuit boards in the first place, and it came up with an answer. Now a very thin coating of low-solids flux (a soldering agent) is applied in a precise pattern so that the circuit board doesn't have to be cleaned before shipping. This innovation has saved AT&T money by eliminating a full stage in the manufacturing process.

The chemical industry has developed some interesting new

processes and practices over the last five years, one of which is the Material Safety Data Sheet (MSDS), which documents each separate chemical being handled in a single process. A copy of this standardized form is provided to each person handling the materials: employees, customers, suppliers, transport companies and, as a good will gesture, regulators and the public as well. The MSDS explains what each chemical is, what its dangers are, what the toxic effect might be and how to handle a spill. This makes accidents much less likely, since in a minor spill or a major disaster inadequate attention to detail and poor communication are always major causal factors.

Four Seasons Hotels & Resorts had an incentive beyond its commitment to greening that encouraged it to alter its waste disposal practices. Waste disposal fees per guest per year were getting out of hand—from a low of US$115 for its Austin, Texas property, to a high of US$998 for Boston, Massachusetts. In 1988, the company spent CDN$933,000 on waste disposal alone; in 1989 the figure had climbed to $1,130,500—a 22 percent increase—while the amount of waste generated remained roughly the same. The company responded by modifying the way it disposes of garbage. Paper, newspapers, glass, aluminum and cardboard is now recycled at most properties, and such measures will be in place at all locations by the end of 1991. The recycling of food waste, which represents 35 percent of a hotel's total waste stream, is being investigated as well. At its newest properties, the company is even designing special rooms to be used as recycling depots.

In some industries, the problem is most often not the product, but the process. One final example illustrates this point. Polystyrene, one of the most ungreen products on the market, is criticized chiefly for its use of CFCs in the manufacturing process. Dow Chemical modified its polystyrene insulation—the company now uses a benign alternative, non-fully halogenated hydrochlorocarbons—and has reduced its reliance on CFCs by 90 percent. Dow's insulation market share has been resuscitated by this single process modification.

Process modification is an important part of the rethinking of industrial processes that typifies the greenest companies. While a modification may be expensive to develop as a result of equipment costs or the difficulty of finding the right suppliers or recycling partners, such practices are highly cost-effective in the long run. Make sure that process modification opportunities are identified as part of your environmental audit.

Redesign Equipment

Equipment redesign has always been a characteristic of technological progress; it is now an integral part of the green business revolution. It includes innovations to emit fewer pollutants to the atmosphere (often recapturing the former pollutant as a reusable by-product), to use fewer resources, raw materials or less energy and to reduce the possibility of hazardous incidents. Many companies see equipment redesign as more than an excellent way to clean up their own act. It is also a way to increase your competitiveness and create new opportunities in the marketplace. E.B. Eddy President E.F. Boswell puts it this way: "The pulp and paper market is tough right now, and we're watching our competitors struggle to introduce new technology in tight times. We saw the writing on the wall and introduced these same measures over a number of years."

New market opportunities are also possible, and interesting partnerships are developing in the field of environmentally friendly equipment. TransAlta Utilities Corporation, Alberta's largest electric utility, worked with Rockwell International to design the LNS coal burner. This burner uses a mixture of air and fuel to reduce acid emissions by 75 to 80 percent; it also surpasses government regulations and has worldwide sales potential.

Even small changes can make a big difference. 3M redesigned a resin spray booth that had been annually responsible for nearly 500,000 pounds of overspray, which could only be disposed of in a special toxic-waste incinerator. When equipment that eliminated the excess spray was installed, toxic emissions were reduced, less resin was required for the same procedure and the company now saves an average of US$125,000 annually on a one-time $45,000 investment.

Significant opportunities exist for companies that are willing to go out on a green limb by investing in new equipment. Innovations such as double-walled storage containers and transmission pipes will soon be included as a standard cost of doing business. In turn, they will significantly reduce the likelihood of a toxic release incident. "Would Exxon have had to pay out billions after the *Valdez* spill if its tankers had been double hulled?" Patrick asks. Asking such questions is the job of the green executive, who must also allocate sufficient resources to evaluate the company's equipment for its redesign potential.

Reformulate

Can a product be made from less toxic materials? Can it be reformulated to use fewer resources, including the energy required in its manufacture? Is it possible to modify it so that it can be disposed of more efficiently—by making it recyclable, for example? More and more companies are asking their research scientists to answer questions like these ones. The answers are often simpler than expected.

"When Loblaws began to recycle its solid wastes there was one item that stumped us," recalls Patrick, "—the waxed cardboard boxes used to ship meat and produce to stores." The solution required a little lateral thinking and a meeting with suppliers. "We discussed the issue with the carton manufacturers, who came up with an alternative product for us in very short order. Now the meat and produce are shipped in a thin plastic bag inside the cardboard box; both containers can be recycled, and our waste disposal costs were reduced by CDN$40,000 a year."

Many products—from packaging to paints—are now being reformulated to eliminate their environmentally damaging components. One type of reformulation that has a great deal of potential is the development of a product that requires less of the raw material that is its major component. This is what E.B. Eddy and other paper manufacturers have done with a technique known as "lightweighting." The result is a paper that is of the same quality and performs as well as the product it replaces, but which uses 25 percent less pulp to produce. This single reformulation has saved the company money, decreased the pressure on our forests and reduced the volume of paper waste.

In the next four to five years product reformulation developments in the petroleum and chemical sectors are expected to escalate rapidly. These will include everything from automobile paint to agricultural fertilizers. The reformulation questions that the greenest companies are asking will soon become standard practice. We recommend you start asking them now.

Save Energy

Energy efficiency programs were one of the hottest ideas when the environmental movement got underway thirty years ago. During the OPEC oil crisis, North American oil companies discovered some of the enormous untapped potential for energy conservation in industry, but many of the savings were temporary. When oil prices fell, there was a tendency to return to the old, wasteful ways.

Today, improved energy management is a largely untapped source of revenue for most companies. The Electric Power Research Institute in Palo Alto, California, estimates that energy-saving techniques could save 24 to 44 percent of the total U.S. demand for electricity by the year 2000. Much of Japanese industry has already adopted energy management measures, and the country currently uses only one-half the energy per unit of GDP that North American industry uses. Research indicates that money invested in introducing such measures can be recouped in two to three years. Why, then, is industry not rushing to institute improved energy management throughout its operations? The simple answer is that such measures require an investment of management time and capital, something not all companies are willing to underwrite.

Pacific Gas and Electric (PG&E) has recognized the growing interest in energy conservation and is investing US$2 billion over ten years to introduce conservation measures to its corporate and residential customers. As part of the company's service, a representative will tour a plant to assess the energy-saving opportunities it presents. PG&E will then subsidize and supervise the installation of efficiency measures throughout the operation, and will provide training and management support. The utility saves money by encouraging energy efficiency which means they do not need to invest in new power-generating capacity, the most costly part of operating a utility. Although PG&E is meeting little resistance from its more conservative customers, it may find the market even easier in a tight economy. With better energy management many businesses could cut their energy use in half and see all those savings go straight to the bottom line within a year or so. During tough economic times, especially, it is simply easier to generate cash by increasing profits than by trying to increase sales.

We believe that energy management is an idea whose time has come in North America and that it will be equally important in every sector, including the service sector. Four Seasons Hotels & Resorts introduced an energy conservation program through its entire hotel group. In the first year of operation, it saved CDN$1.5 million, and the savings continue to grow as new ideas are introduced. The company's newest hotel, near San Diego, California, uses electricity during the inexpensive evening hours to manufacture a refrigerator room full of ice. This ice is then used to cool the facilities during the day.

The transportation sector will be one of the biggest winners in the field of energy management. British Airways has had a comprehensive computerized energy management system in place at Heathrow and Gatwick airports since 1988. The airline calculates that it saved over US$5 million in energy bills in the ensuing two-year period.

In short, make the search for energy savings a priority. If you don't, you will be left scrambling to catch up as energy costs rapidly increase throughout the coming decade.

In cleaning up the plant, many companies now set themselves the goal of zero emissions and zero waste. While this goal is no more attainable than the goal of zero defects in product manufacture, it serves a similar purpose: to set the highest possible standard of excellence. Cleaning up the plant won't be easy, but it will help you gain an increasing share of the green marketplace.

The Neighborhood

Cleaning up your act will be popular with the communities in which you operate and will help defuse potential local opposition to your plans. It will be even more popular if it extends to areas of local concern, such as soil contamination. This means rectifying your past mistakes as well as your current practices, an activity that can be very expensive. But such actions are an important first step toward establishing good community relations; they are justifiably regarded as "doing the right thing for the right reason." "Cleaning up the neighbourhood gives a triple advantage," says Roger Hewitt, managing director of Shanks and McEwan, a U.K. waste contractor. "It improves community relations and helps the company win future planning permission, and impresses investors that the company is going to use its funds responsibly." It may even win you some positive publicity. Eastman Gelatine Corporation's clean-up of five spent-lime storage basins cost them US$3 million. But when the company sealed, capped and covered the basins, the American Council for Consulting Engineers of New England presented it with an award for engineering excellence. As an additional bonus for such virtuous behavior, both the American and the Canadian governments provide a variety of tax incentives for companies to reduce their impact on the local environment or in some way improve the community in which they are active.

Cleaning up your own backyard is an important part of being a good neighbor—and one of the most popular ways of doing this is by managing greenspaces around your company's facilities or on other lands owned by your firm. Greenspaces are increasingly seen as having great value, and many cities are developing tough regulations concerning the clean up of unoccupied privately-owned land, so it is to your advantage to find out how you can turn your land into a public asset. Some companies take a back-to-nature approach after developing an alliance with the Wildlife Habitat Enhancement Council, which helps firms green their properties. As a result of this cooperation, companies are putting unoccupied real estate holdings to good use—as nature reserves. Nests for endangered terns were built close to ponds of purified water near Amoco's chemical plant in South Carolina; Monsanto includes the enhancement of wetland areas in its land reclamation projects (wetland near its Tennessee plant has become home to one and a half million trees and thousands of birds); and fourteen sites that IBM once intended for future development (about ten thousand acres in eight U.S. states) are currently being restored as natural grasslands. In this last project, the company is planting wild grasses, wildflowers, trees and hedgerows to prevent soil erosion and restore the land's natural balance. But no project is too small. The Council reports that since 1978 they have helped a Baltimore financial services firm, USF&G, maintain a three by eight foot nesting area on a ledge of its downtown offices.

One of the principles of neighborhood greening is that environmental considerations must be an important part of any proposed development. The development of the Alyeska trans-Alaska pipeline is an early example of this principle in action. Constructed in 1977 at a cost of US$9 million, it included gravel ramps so that caribou could walk across the pipeline and sections built on stilts so that animals could walk underneath it. After construction, Alyeska replanted the area along the route, since

Arctic plants are slow to regenerate.

The NIMBY phenomenon is not about to go away. Sooner or later one of your operations will face some sort of community protest. But you can avoid most of these problems by writing neighborhood greening into your corporate green strategy.

Your Industry

In the summer of 1990 BASF, Exxon, Dow Chemical, General Electric, Goodyear, Occidental, Reichold, Texaco and Texas Petro-Chemical pledged to reduce overall annual emissions of pollutants by 83 percent by 1991. In the fall of the previous year AT&T, The Boeing Company, Digital Equipment Corporation, Ford Motor Company, General Electric, Honeywell, Motorola, Northern Telecom and Texas Instruments announced the formation of a new organization to reduce and eliminate CFC use. There are many other examples of this kind of inter-industry cooperation, and we believe that this is a sign of things to come. Often individual companies recognize that there are advantages in working on environmental projects with other enterprises affected by the same issues. These rewards include shared knowledge, expertise and cost. Cooperation also gives larger companies a chance to assist smaller companies for whom greening represents a managerial mountain and who may not have the resources to make the changes on their own. Cooperation between firms is really of mutual benefit, as the impact of one company's greening is diminished if no other companies follow suit. Working together, as Patrick has discovered from his own experience, "these groups can be powerful lobbying organizations."

The greening of whole sectors is being spearheaded by industry associations that are busy developing the best environmental practices. The Canadian Chemical Manufacturing Association's (CMA) "Responsible Care" program, for instance, ensures that its members operate safely. The program stipulates codes of practice that include such measures as prompt reporting of chemical-related health and environmental hazards, specific methods for reducing emissions and standards for emergency planning. Companies must join the Responsible Care program as a condition of membership in the CMA. Responsible Care has been picked up by the the American chemical industry and is being imitated by other industry associations as well, as business moves to ensure that a standard approach is taken to environmental care.

One of the most pressing of current environmental issues, the landfill shortage, convinced manufacturers, packagers and retailers that they needed to begin to work together to contribute to a solution. The most successful strategy such alliances have adopted is the development of residential recycling programs. The coalition partners recognized that these programs would not only reduce community and government opposition to their products and reduce the amount of solid waste going to landfills, but would also create a whole new resource base. In 1965, long before most North American companies had thought about environmental problems, Reynolds Aluminum launched a municipal recycling program, which has served as a model for other community schemes. In the last three years, the idea has become more popular partly in response to growing awareness of the landfill crisis and partly due to regulatory pressures (which are a direct result of the crisis).

In Ontario in 1988 an association formed by six soft-drink manufacturers and their container suppliers (known as Ontario Multi-Material Recycling Incorporated—OMMRI), made a CDN$20 million commitment over four years toward the development of a municipal-residential recycling program that is now regarded as the best in the world. OMMRI's members were under pressure from government to reduce the amount of waste generated by their products, and they devised this scheme as a solution. The association did not restrict itself to soft-drink bottles, however; it also aimed to substantially reduce the amount of household waste going to landfills. Here is how the system works: Each household is given a free, sturdy, blue plastic box, known as a Blue Box. These boxes are used by householders to collect recyclables, including glass bottles and jars, steel and aluminum food and beverage containers, plastic soft-drink bottles and newspapers. One day each week the reusable Blue Boxes are placed at curbside for pickup by special recycling trucks. The program, which couldn't have gotten started without OMMRI's financial support, has achieved householder participation levels far beyond expectations and a significant reduction in the amount of waste going to landfill, prompting inquiries from cities all over North America. "I am continually asked about Ontario's Blue Box program," Patrick notes, "and I tell people it's a model case of business seizing the environmental initiative."

We believe that cleaning up your act is the most important investment your company will make in the next few years. As you move through the various stages of greening you will undoubtedly discover new business opportunities and come up with ideas for new products and services. In the next chapter we look at the basics of researching environmental innovations for the North American marketplace.

□ FIVE □

Research and Develop Green Products and Services

Green is a word that came into common usage in Europe in the 1980s to describe a product that is "environmentally improved." How does this apply to the real world of goods and services? In the simplest terms, the less harm a product or service does to the planet, the greener it is. The perfect green product doesn't deplete a nonrenewable resource or damage the earth's environmental capital at any stage in its life cycle. Is such a perfect product possible? Natural spring water in reusable bottles? Perhaps, but what does the extraction of millions of gallons of water do to the water table? In truth, our very existence on the planet means that we will have some kind of negative impact on our natural environment. The best a green product or service can hope to do—at this point—is to cause less harm than its competition, but even a minor improvement can translate into a major increase in sales.

Such a product may, for example, contain a smaller amount of raw material or fewer toxic elements. It may require less energy to manufacture, to transport or to use. It may create less waste or be easily recyclable or even be safe to dump in a landfill. It may simply last longer or have less packaging. It may be easier to repair or be reusable instead of disposable. "Green" is still a loosely defined term, and the definition of what is green is changing almost daily. One of the greatest challenges green pioneers now face is to develop products that are truly green and that won't be obsolete next week.

This chapter aims to guide you through the process of green product and service research and development, so that you can improve your company's image and increase its market share. Our primary focus here is the sector made up of enterprises that manufacture consumer goods, and businesses that sell directly to the public. These organizations are most sensitive to the radical shift in consumer consciousness that is now taking place, and they are actively trying to anticipate where the tastes of the new green shopper are heading. This is clearly a growth sector: Marketing Intelligence Service Ltd. reports that there were more new green products introduced in the United States in the first half of 1990 (308) than in all of 1989 (262).

However, the impact of the green consumer is not limited to companies close to the retail end of the spectrum. Consider this simple scenario, some elements of which are already happening. Faced with overcrowded landfills and the rising cost of garbage, cities across North America start to charge their citizens for garbage pick up at a price per bag. As a result, city residents look for ways to reduce the amount of garbage they throw away. They demand and get comprehensive curbside recycling programs, which in turn puts increasing pressure on retailers to sell products that can be easily recycled. And they start to look at the amount of packaging they buy. They complain about all the excess packaging. Some irate customers even tear it off the products and leave it in the aisles. Retailers get the message and insist that manufacturers stop using certain types of packaging. They refuse to stock certain wasteful products, an action that sends shock waves right back down the line all the way to the forest and petroleum sectors that provide the raw resources for most packaging.

This is what the Environmental Defence Fund refers to as "the ripple effect" of green consumerism, and it is beginning to be felt by companies far behind the front lines, just as the domino effect of companies cleaning up their internal operations reverberates along the whole network of customers and suppliers. The ripple effect encompasses the entire business continuum, including the whole range of enterprises, where much buying and selling takes place from business to business. The green consumer is now knocking on everyone's door.

Therefore, if you are considering developing a green product or service, you will need to have an understanding of green marketing trends and how they will affect the products you wish to sell. Robert Murray, Colgate-Palmolive's corporate communications director puts it this way: "Yes, it's a competitive edge to say you have a green product, but first we had to discover what a green product was and how to promote it as such." Green market research, green product research and developing green packaging differ from what you've been used to. They involve new ideas such as "cradle-to-grave" product assessments. "Consumers and environmental groups don't expect companies to have all the answers," Patrick believes. "But they do expect you to do *something*, and selling greenery is tough, mainly because we're all making up the rules as we go along. One thing is clear: companies that sell green with the same glitz as the rest of their product lines will ultimately fail."

Green research and development is still in its infancy and the experts are only beginning to catch up with the fundamental shift in societal values that is causing the best green products to sell so well. Most companies are still struggling to view the marketplace through green-tinted glasses. Old ways of thinking die hard, even among marketing types. It's true that many of the facts involved in research and development for the green market are the same as those affecting conventional market research and product development. The demographic make up of the North American population didn't change dramatically between 1987 (the beginning of green consumerism here) and early 1991, when this book went to press. What has changed is the way green companies look at these facts and interpret them. In other words, the best green research and development is coming from the companies that have shifted their way of thinking along the lines we've been describing in the preceding chapters.

A few companies, Loblaws among them, have begun the long and complex job of taking advantage of the green market. They realize that they are at the investment stage, and that while research and development is very expensive up front, it pays off in the long run. To use a pioneer analogy they have sent out prospectors and surveyors and begun to map out this new territory, to build the first roads and construct the first settlements. But much of the land is still wilderness and many of the roads still don't have signs. It is therefore all the more important to be a green marketing pioneer and to move in faster than your competitors. As already stated, the reasons to go green are multiple: your consumer demands it, government regulations require it, and your smartest competitors are already frantically working on it. In summary the benefits can be enormous both to your balance sheet and corporate image—if you do your homework.

Green Market Research

The essence of all market research is to obtain precise, accurate and up-to-date information. However, there are three types of information that are crucial to green market research:

1. the most current information on regulatory developments, which will determine what can go into your product

2. detailed information about the needs of increasingly sophisticated green consumers and what they want
3. high-quality analyses of market trends: what your competitors are doing or planning to do, and how green products are selling and what the next wave of products will look like

According to Patrick, "Green market research is a little bit like a jigsaw puzzle—all the pieces are there, but you can't find the lid of the box to see what the whole picture looks like." Most marketers agree that green marketing is different from what they've been practicing. How is it different? The skills required to target and understand this consumer are the same as those used in traditional market research but the values of the "quarry" are so new, so totally different compared to anything we have seen before, and they are changing so rapidly that some research tools may be in greater demand than others. The green marketer needs a solid sociological and psychological profile of the green consumer and the choices this new consumer is making—and this information must be updated much more frequently than has been the case for other market research studies. This is, after all, a green *revolution*; its victors will be companies with the best sources of intelligence.

Keep Ahead of Product Regulations

This aspect of green market research is simply an outgrowth of your ongoing monitoring of what government regulators are currently doing or planning to do. And that means not only keeping a close watch on the regulators themselves (lobbying where appropriate), but also keeping a careful eye on the various interest groups that influence regulators, especially environmental organizations. Any contacts you have established with the kind of groups described in Chapter Two will prove very valuable here, as will the services of an environmental consultant. Hot environmental issues soon translate into regulations; these people know what's hot and getting hotter. There are two areas here to which you should be particularly attentive: (1) regulations that affect the contents of a product, and (2) regulations that affect what you can put on the label. In both these areas there are current developments you should be aware of.

Product content regulations are changing quickly and getting tougher. Regulations concerning what can go into landfills are changing—and you will need to keep abreast of such developments, because they will determine what goes into your product and package. In Ontario, for example, regulations will forbid the dumping of glass, cardboard and metals into landfills as of April 1, 1991. Proposals in several U.S. states have tackled the landfill problem by suggesting a tax on packaging, based on its recyclability and recycled content. Massachusetts and Oregon are considering a requirement that packaging be either reusable, recyclable or made of recycled content. Naturally, manufacturers are concerned about this kind of development: if one state banned a material and the next state banned another, how could companies sell their goods across the country? In the European Community pending legislation would require 70 percent of all packaging to be either recyclable or refillable, and similar restrictions are expected to follow in North America. As always, the best policy is to develop products that are ahead of the regulators.

A direct outgrowth of stricter regulations is the banning of certain products because they contain or are packaged in something that is considered to be harmful to the environment. Such product bans are growing, and some are highly questionable. While most would not argue with the recent Environmental Protection Agency decision to ban mercury in latex paint, the pros and cons are much less clear in other cases. Often the ban is a knee-jerk reaction to increased activism, fueled by a landfill shortage and fanned by provocative media coverage. The two most prominent targets of the new banning fervor are polystyrene packaging and disposable diapers. Proponents of these bans want to replace polystyrene with paper, but have failed to prove that paper, which doesn't degrade with any certainty in a landfill, is an improvement. As for replacing disposable diapers with cloth, a paper delivered to the International Recycling Congress concluded that cloth and disposables had about the same environmental impact when you consider factors such as the detergent and energy used in laundering, and the energy used in transportation. In short, bans may be based on superficial analysis, and so be poorly conceived and inconsistent, but you would still be wise to anticipate them, and you can only do this by keeping on top of environmental issues.

The second regulatory area that you should monitor constantly is what you can say on a label. At the moment there are no government-imposed environmental labeling standards in place in Canada or the United States, but it is merely a matter of time before such regulations are put in place. They will set down strict definitions of such terms as "environmently friendly," "recycled," "recyclable," "biodegradable" and "green." A new report released by a task force of the American State Attorneys General recommends the development of government standards and definitions for green terms so that "business will know what to do in order to make specific environmental claims." The Canadian department of consumer and corporate affairs is taking similar action. However, consumers are already demanding that what you claim about a product, either in advertising or on the label be provable. As a result we recommend that you be prepared to fully back up any claims that you make. We also suggest that you get involved in one of North America's voluntary eco-labeling schemes. You'll find more information on this important development in the packaging section later in this chapter.

Targeting the New Green Consumer

The single most important activity you can engage in while researching the market for green products and services is to improve your knowledge and understanding of the new green consumer. You already know green consumers are changing

North American buying habits, but how well do you understand how these consumers think, what they want in a green product and what kind of premium—if any—they are willing to pay for green? These are the kinds of questions you need to answer in order to refine your products in such a way that they will reach this lucrative target market. "Bear in mind that eco-consumerism is a moving target," Patrick admonishes. "You can't research the issue to death if you want to increase your share of the market. Loblaws' success was due mainly to everyone working around the clock. The competition didn't have time to react."

There are a number of concrete steps you can take to add to your raw data about these consumers. We've already talked about some of them: reading and analyzing what is in the broad selection of green consumer guides, for example. As with regulators, consumers are highly sensitive to the environmental issue of the moment. If glass is about to be banned from municipal landfills across the nation, and most communities don't yet have recycling programs in place, think twice about selling your new organically grown baby-carrots in a glass jar. If automobiles that can't use alternative fuels are about to be banned from Southern California—your largest market—you'll have to quickly consider retooling your production lines.

Sometimes you have more information at your fingertips than you realize. One of the first things Patrick did when Loblaws decided to develop its green product line was to go back and read the mail the company had been getting from its customers. Consumers' requests could be summarized in two words: less and more; less packaging and more environmentally friendly content. "One helpful customer said that she had just switched to Loblaws from a competitor," Patrick recalls. "She was writing to say that she wholeheartedly supported our G.R.E.E.N product line. But she also enclosed a rather large box full of the packaging she'd collected from her week's shopping, and she asked us if there wasn't anything we could do about reducing it." Letters like that told him a great deal about the kinds of products that would be welcomed and how to present them.

During 1991 we expect to see a number of green marketing guides launched in North America. Already available is *Green MarketAlert*, a survey and analysis of green trends published by Connecticut-based MarketAlert Publications. Launched in 1990, this monthly has already proven to be a valuable tool for green marketers. In Canada, Southam Business Information and Communications has announced *The Canadian Green Marketing Guide* (due in 1991) which will be updated quarterly. These guides are the most up-to-date sources of information we know of on subjects such as changing consumer attitudes, environmental advertising and promotion, forthcoming government regulations and innovative green marketing ideas.

However, the single most useful tool of green marketing research is the in-depth opinion survey. If you can afford to, you should be polling green consumers on a regular basis. If you can't, you should be subscribing to one of the annual surveys conducted by the leading opinion samplers in North America. Every polling company is doing this kind of sampling of green consumer opinion. And the ones that have been published so far reveal a remarkably consistent profile of who this green consumer is.

For one thing, the polls agree that green consumers cut across all demographic lines. They come from all social groups, all economic classes, all ages and regions. Although pollsters vary in their estimates of the size of the green consumer market, the general consensus is that at least 60 percent of North Americans are concerned about the environment and factor green into their purchasing decisions. (Some surveys put the figure as high as 85 percent.) Interestingly, green consumers are generally optimistic about the chances that the environment will improve over the next twenty to thirty years; analysts conclude that this is in part due to a widely held belief that new consumption habits and a growing concern about the environment will lead to significant and lasting changes. Most pollsters also believe that the evidence indicates a probable narrowing of the gap between attitudes and behavior as green issues become a larger part of North American life. Interestingly, public pressure for tough regulatory action is at its highest level since green consumer surveys began in 1986. We note that this enthusiasm might be tempered if all manufacturers do not respond as the green pioneers have.

Things get even more interesting once these surveys attempt to break the green consumer sector into subgroups. Take, for example, a recent survey of Canadian consumers by the Angus Reid Group, one of the country's most respected polling firms. The findings split Canadians into seven segments based on their environmental points of view: the greenest consumers comprise 63 percent of the population: of these 19 percent are optimists, 16 percent are enthusiasts, 15 percent are activists and 12 percent are anxious. The rest include fatalists at 15 percent, the apathetic at 13 percent and the hostile at 9 percent.

Clearly, public awareness of environmental issues is translating into some strongly held opinions. And as this new sense of social responsibility grows, it is beginning to color purchasing decisions. The J. Walter Thompson USA advertising agency reports that nearly 50 percent of North Americans have taken some kind of green consumer action, whether by reading a product label for environmentally harmful ingredients or by buying a product they believed was better for the environment. Polls can tell you what green consumers are concerned about and how those concerns relate to your product; they may even suggest what changes could be made to make your product greener.

Not surprisingly, the key concerns of green consumers are often those that have been regularly reported by the press. This means, for example, that people seem unconcerned about the idea of waste reduction at source, a concept that currently gets little publicity; in fact many consumers are not even sure what the term means. Of course, an astute marketer might take this lack of knowledge as a challenge and develop an ad campaign that would educate the green consumer about source reduction and promote his company's product at the same time.

Finally, opinion polls provide some clues as to how much consumers are willing to pay for greener products. Reports vary, but on average 32 percent of North American consumers say they will pay more for a greener product, as long as it works. In general, they don't want to trade down when they buy something environmentally friendly: they want the same quality and performance as in the product they are accustomed to buying. Dishwasher detergent is an excellent example of this principle in action. While phosphate-free laundry detergents have been very successful, dishwasher detergents that have been similarly greened are not, according to the droves of consumers who are returning these products to stores for refunds. The bottom line is that it has to work, or its greenness is no advantage at all.

At the moment, most green products are more expensive than the products they are designed to replace. Research and development costs are high, and the products often cost more to produce, because they are usually manufactured in smaller quantities. An example of this is the chicken produced by Canada's Roth Family Farms, which is fed organically grown grain from the American Midwest. This grain costs up to 70 percent more than standard feedstock and as a result, the product must be also be sold at a premium price. As with other goods and services, as markets and supply expand, the prices will inevitably come down.

The more clearly you see the green consumer's profile, the more able you will be to develop products that are acceptable to his or her new tastes.

Market Trends: What Your Competitors Are Doing

Your market research is not complete until you find out what your competitors are planning or already have in the pipeline. The green marketing guides we referred to earlier attempt to pinpoint some of these trends, and will be able to provide you with regular surveys of the latest developments. But in most instances the best information is the data you gather and interpret for your own market segment.

Don't forget that your own staff can be a valuable resource: ask them what they are buying or what they would like to see in the marketplace or what they have read about that is available in other regions or other countries. Send your researchers to investigate what other retailers are selling: if you are a drugstore chain, what can you learn from grocery retailers and vice versa? Europe is always a good place to look for trends. IBM has recognized the North American potential in product recycling as a customer-service strategy because in the European Community, the company has for several years been asked to take back used computers and parts. Now the U.S. parent is investigating the possibility of launching a similar program in North America. Product disposal as part of a sales package is sure to be one of the key new services of the 1990s.

Here is a preliminary survey of the green products and services that sold well—to both consumers and business—in 1990.

1. *Toilet tissue made from recycled pulp.* The key seems to be that this product is virtually indistinguishable from and provides the same quality and service as toilet paper made from virgin fibres.

2. *Baking soda.* Once a low-profile staple in grocery stores and in kitchen cupboards, baking soda experienced a rebirth as an environmentally friendly cleaner, silver polish, drain cleaner and bathwater addition. This is a great example of a product that was inherently green and needed only to be labeled as such.

3. *Nonchlorinated pulp products.* Whiter-than-white was once perceived as an important added-value for products such as disposable diapers and sanitary napkins. Now that public concern about dioxins and furans in bleached pulp has peaked, chlorine-free pulp is gaining acceptance. In some European countries, it is already the rule rather than the exception. Where available in North America, these products do very well. As a result, a new phrase has been coined; "beige is beautiful."

4. *Organic foods,* once limited to the health food market, are

now served in the best restaurants in town, and sold in many supermarkets. Demand for organic produce and meats in North America exceeds supply.

5. *Recycled paper* is being produced by most of the major paper companies across the continent and is not only being sold to many large businesses but to all levels of government.

6. *Vegetable-based inks and dyes* have become the preferred choice for green printing houses, as an alternative to chemical-based products. In particular, many of the labels on green products use these new inks.

7. *Bottled water* sales have increased dramatically in the past three years. In 1989, the Canadian market was worth more than CDN$100 million, and Americans paid out $2 billion plus for purified or spring water. The huge volume of sales was due primarily to public concern generated by reports about the quality of municipal tap water.

8. *Unbleached coffee filters* are another item on the long list of unbleached paper goods that are capturing public attention. Even the largest coffee filter company in the world—Germany's Melitta—has moved to satisfy its consumer demand for natural, environmentally safe products.

9. *Re-refined motor oil* was one of the first products to receive the eco-label in a number of different countries—it continues to be a very popular product with environmentalists and consumers alike. Oil doesn't wear out, it only gets dirty. Recapturing and cleaning it means a reduced requirement for a nonrenewable resource and prevents millions of litres of used motor oil from being dumped into sewage systems.

10. *Energy-efficient lightbulbs* have been an immediate success wherever they are introduced. Although they are more expensive than standard incandescent bulbs, they last ten times longer, and use 75 percent less energy.

Now that you've surveyed the green marketplace by looking at regulations, consumer trends, what your competitors are up to and what's selling, what does all of this mean to your company? It means you are more informed about how to begin developing green products and services. K-Mart Australia, which launched a line of green products that was very successful with its customers, has this advice to offer companies: Before you introduce an environmental program, make sure that you are aware of your own policies and procedures, and their impact on the environment; wrestle with the complex issue of what comprises an environmentally positive product and ensure that your products do one of three things: (1) encourage people to conserve, (2) reduce consumption or (3) encourage recycling or reuse.

Develop Green Products

In January 1989 Loblaws launched one of the most secret and intensive corporate label development projects ever. It was carried out with the greatest urgency and under the most secret conditions. "We were adamant that we would be the first in the Canadian marketplace with a line of green consumer products," Patrick remembers, "and in order to do this we had to move quickly and to keep what we were doing under close wraps. One small leak to the press could mean that months of preparation would be for naught." One of the first responsibilities of the project team was to do some general research on what the new green consumer wanted. This included much of what we suggested earlier in this chapter—such as developing an understanding of the green consumer, investigating product regulations and so on—and the team extended their search beyond Canada's borders, into the United States, Europe and beyond. The genesis of many products came from underdeveloped countries. They read every letter sent to the company in the previous eighteen months. They attended trade shows, visited their competitors' supermarkets and surveyed specialty stores and health food shops where greener products had been sold for years. Meanwhile, they pored over the existing green consumer guides from Britain and other countries and compared notes about what they discovered while investigating other products for the "President's Choice" and "No Name" lines.

The team developed insight into the most pressing environmental issues of the day with the help of Pollution Probe, the Toronto-based environmental group they had brought on board to assist in the product development process. "Many of the products we needed to develop were sitting right on the shelves of our own stores," Patrick admits. "Once we knew, for example, that the phosphate in detergents was a serious environmental issue, a walk down the supermarket aisle told us there was no nationally advertised phosphate-free soap powder. And when we discovered that the paper-bleaching process leaves traces of toxic chemicals in the finished product, we knew there was a market niche for unbleached coffee filters." To help them spot these opportunities, Loblaws invited Pollution Probe and its executive director, Colin Isaacs, to perform an environmental analysis of the company's supermarkets in order to select products that Loblaws could reasonably develop and sell as green.

Spotting the opportunity was only the first step; developing the products proved to be the more difficult aspect of Loblaws' sprint into the green marketplace. Instead of simply repackaging something that was already available, in some instances the company had to start from scratch. Other products were being manufacturered for small markets elsewhere—for North American specialty stores—but Loblaws had to find each product, approve its content and packaging, locate a satisfactory manufacturer, repackage the product and ensure that sufficient quantities could be guaranteed to meet the demands of a nationally advertised product line.

In addition to Pollution Probe's knowledge, another reason for bringing this environmenal group on board was that Probe agreed to endorse individual products in the green line if these products satisfied the group's basic green criteria. These criteria included the following: less raw material used in manufacture, the elimination of a toxic component standard in competing brands and use of recycled materials in the product or package. Loblaws believed this endorsement would help validate its products in the public's mind. In return, the company agreed to pay the environmental group up to CDN$75,000 over the life of the agreement, based on sales of the green product line.

One word of caution here. As we discussed in Chapter Two, entering into any alliance with an environmental group is a decision that must not be made casually. Make sure at the outset that you understand the group's objectives and how it intends to work with you. Make sure as well that your own standards and goals are made perfectly clear. It is important to get these really basic matters sorted out in the beginning, so that both sides are speaking the same language. Don't forget that when the product a group endorses is launched its reputation is on the line. Destroy its credibility and you destroy your own, thereby defeating the entire exercise.

The purpose of the Pollution Probe analysis was twofold: to identify products that were already green and simply required repositioning, and to suggest greener alternatives to existing products. The first kind of product is exemplified by baking soda. Baking soda is not only a deodorizer, but also an all-round cleanser that meets strict environmental guidelines. Simply put a new package on it, drawing attention to its greenness, put it in the cleaning section of your supermarket and you have—with the minimum of effort—a new green product. The second product type (alternatives to existing items) was often available in other markets, such as specialty stores, and in European groceries, so it was simply a matter of importing or repackaging them, as was the case with unbleached coffee filters. This product was purchased in Sweden, a country that had a number of years previously introduced legislation requiring paper manufacturers to dramatically reduce the use of chlorine as a bleaching agent and where a number of household goods were therefore available in unbleached form. For several products, however, no green alternative existed, but it seemed possible to develop one.

Pollution Probe's "green comb," as Colin Isaacs called this audit process, identified eight products that it would consider endorsing: re-refined motor oil, phosphate-free laundry detergent, phosphate-free dish detergent, unbleached disposable diapers, unbleached sanitary napkins and three gardening products: organic fertilizer, natural topsoil dressing and a soil conditioner made from wood pulp waste.

As Loblaws' experience demonstrates, developing green products can be a very complicated process. If you decide against entering into a formal relationship with an environmental group, you should consult widely before you determine the products and market you wish to develop. In general, we recommend that you draw on all the outside expertise available in producing the greenest products possible. In Loblaws' case, consultations were restricted to Pollution Probe and its suppliers, which allowed Loblaws to keep the entire project confidential. But even if secrecy is one of your objectives, which is a given with most companies, you can throw a wide net at the beginning of your enquiries and close ranks when you get closer to the details of your product or service's development. Obviously, the more information you have, the more likely you are to develop a product the green consumer will buy.

The essential elements to successful green product development are no different from those followed in the development of any successful commercial item. They are (1) what goes into the product and (2) how it will be packaged. Ascertain what its environmental impact will be and the way it is likely to be perceived by a green and sophisticated audience. As with every stage of turning your company green, environmental product development requires a new way of thinking. Although the product and its package go through a similar development process, we've kept them separate so that the important differences can be highlighted.

Greening the Product

As Loblaws' deal with Pollution Probe proved, moderate environmental groups don't insist on a flawlessly green product before they will endorse it. Such groups want to see products that are environmentally superior to what is currently in the marketplace, which means that they are willing to make reasonable compromises. None of the initial eight items in the line was perfectly green, but both Pollution Probe and Loblaws believed each was a step in the right direction.

Green Product Criteria

It should be clear by now that green standards are rising—among both consumers and regulators. Therefore, the greener your product is, the greater the chance of its acceptability. Increasingly, consumers want manufacturers and retailers to make the composition and performance of their products more transparent, which means they want to know everything about a product during its entire life cycle. But as the success of Loblaws' G.R.E.E.N line shows, any significant environmental improvement over existing products is a marketing plus.

The next question to pose when developing a green product is: "What are the key criteria of green product development?" We think that there are three. They are:

1. How green is green enough?
2. Where in the product's life cycle should you concentrate your development dollars?
3. How does your new green product compare to the ungreen product you want it to displace?

The first criterion of green product development is to set yourself a goal based on your market research. Decide how green to make your product based on what is already on the market and what you believe consumers want. This is what Loblaws did in the case of soap powder. Phosphates are added to most laundry detergents to boost their cleaning power. But phosphates have also been generating some negative publicity because even relatively small amounts can rapidly overfertilize a body of water. This enrichment promotes the growth of algae, and excess algae can result in the suffocation of other aquatic life. Removal of phosphates seemed a natural first choice when developing a greener laundry detergent. There is no doubt that detergents include some other hazards in their life cycle—during their manufacture, use and disposal—but by removing phosphates, Loblaws removed the major environmental objection to laundry detergent, and made its detergent one component greener than that of the competition.

The second criterion is considerably more complex. Deciding where in the life cycle to concentrate your greening depends partly on what kind of product or service you are developing. Let's take another example from the Loblaws line as an example: coffee filters made from unbleached paper. In determining how to make coffee filters greener, Loblaws decided to concentrate again on one of the more public aspects of paper products: the practice of bleaching pulp with chlorine. Environmental groups have claimed for years that such bleaching leaches potentially toxic chlorinated compounds into our waterways and that residues of the by-products of the process, including dioxins and furans, remain in the paper itself. By purchasing filters in Sweden that had been manufactured with paper that had bypassed the bleaching stage (something no North American manufacturer was doing at the time), Loblaws made the product greener.

Eventually, of course, pulp and paper producers will green their processes even further—by making recycled paper with a larger percentage of post-consumer waste, for example. Loblaws might then start to market reusable coffee filters that eliminate the need for disposables altogether. This has been done in another area of green product development: when Loblaws launched its green line, it included disposable diapers made from unbleached pulp. By the end of 1990, the company introduced its line of reusable cloth diapers, even though disposable diapers represent a significant percentage of its revenues.

As we have continually pointed out, consumers are naturally most concerned with the environmental news they are hearing from the media. A label that reads "phosphate-free" has impact because it tells them that the product's contents do not include something they have been told causes pollution. If the label read: "manufactured using less energy" this might also help sales, but it would not seem as immediate or powerful. Surveys show clearly that the average person is more interested in reducing the pollution caused by a product after it is purchased than in reducing pollution at the time it is made or at some earlier point in its life cycle. By buying phosphate-free soap powder consumers know they are reducing water pollution, and this makes them feel good. It comes down to consumer awareness, and savvy on the part of the manufacturer. The key is to determine the impact of changing one element of a product.

Over time consumers will become more concerned about the earlier stages of the life cycle; this will change as consumers become more knowledgeable about the causes of global warming, for instance. In some well-publicized cases, such as tuna caught in driftnets, they already have a high level of awareness. This change will be intensified as products become more "transparent," as the level of general public awareness about the full spectrum of environmental issues increases, and as more and more is known about what makes up each product in the marketplace. But for now this new life cycle rule applies to most green products.

As part of your decision on where to concentrate your greening, pay special attention to the eco-labeling schemes that are under development in your country or in neighboring jurisdictions. Such programs are explicit about what standards green products and packages must satisfy in order to receive the seal of approval. We believe that it is only a matter of years before green labeling schemes will be standard in all industrialized nations and recommend that you take this important new development into consideration when developing your green line. For example, diaper services that wish to receive Canada's privately run Environmental Choice accreditation must (1) specialize in diaper laundering and (2) use antisceptic infection control practices and meet specific criteria regarding bacteria count, pH level, cleaning agents and waste water treatment. When finalized, Environmental Choice guidelines for laundry detergents and cloth diapers will also apply.

The third and final criterion of green product development is complex: How should your new green product compare to the one you want it to displace? Should it look the same, act the same, perform in exactly the same way? The simple answer is this: make it as close as possible to the old product in every way except in environmental impact. Consumers want to help the environment, but they also like the familiar, especially when it works just as well as what they're used to. They don't want a detergent that leaves clothes looking dingy, even if it is greener than the one they have been using. Above all, they don't want to give up the convenience of the products they are used to.

The more complicated answer is: it depends. Compact fluorescent lightbulbs are a good example of how complex green product development can be. These lightbulbs have been available in select markets from small producers for years—and energy management specialists such as Amory Lovins have been extolling their virtues since the 1970s, because they last longer and use much less electricity than their incandescent counterparts. Now, suddenly, compact flourescents are more widely available, but there are still some drawbacks to their design. For example, tubes are longer than standard bulbs and as a result don't fit into many light fixtures. Still, when Loblaws introduced these green lightbulbs in a joint program with the provincial utility Ontario Hydro, they sold out within days. (The utility offered a $5.00 rebate as an incentive.) This is an excellent example of how different industries can work together to satisfy green consumer demands.

The next phase of the green revolution will see companies competing not just to out-green each other, but to develop green products that perform on a par with or better than any of their environmentally damaging equivalents. In some cases, a green product may succeed even if it performs considerably less well than what it replaces. Take the push that is now on to develop an alternative to CFCs. Here's how one European chemical company manager described the situation, "We are going out with a product which is less efficient than the one we are replacing, costs five times as much, and the only reason is because of the environmental imperative. We've never been in a market quite like it before."

The Development Process

Once you have a clear idea of what your intended green product must accomplish, you still have a long way to go. There are three basic stages to this development. These are:

1. do the research
2. produce and test a prototype and
3. refine the product prior to final manufacture in quantity

When you are developing a new green product such as a phosphate-free laundry detergent, your research stage may involve some fairly basic science. Unless you have your own research laboratories, you will have to go outside your organization. Loblaws developed their G.R.E.E.N 100 percent phosphate-free laundry detergent with the help of Pollution Probe and their in-house product development and research team.

The general thrust of green product development, of course, is to manufacture products that have a reduced impact on the environment. Inevitably, there were some false starts. "Biodegradable" plastic bags were one of the earliest green products in the market. But soon after their introduction environmentalists and scientific organizations proved that they were not biodegradable at all, and the claims were withdrawn by the manufacturers and the retailers.

Products that Loblaws calls "body friendly" also fall into the green category: consumers link health issues and environmental concerns when considering what to buy. The Loblaws G.R.E.E.N line includes products that are low-calorie, low-fat, low-cholesterol and high-fiber, such as High-Fibre Corn Flakes. Research into this kind of green product has also become an important part of the environmentally improved marketplace. As Patrick puts it, "Consumers are becoming more concerned about the internal environment." When Canada's Roth Family Farms set out to develop their organic chicken, proprietor Wrex Roth discovered that he could learn much of what he needed to know from history. "While organizations such as the Organic Crop Improvement Association and people such as agricultural college poultry nutritionists were of great help to us," Roth says, "I also talked to my father, my grandfather and some of the older farmers in the area to see how they raised poultry before our modern-day practices of growth hormones and antibiotics." The chickens have been a phenomenal success story across the country, and as the first company in the market, Roth Family Farms enjoys 95 percent of the organic chicken market.

IBM has taken the longest possible view, by requiring that a full life cycle impact audit be completed on each of the products the company manufactures. The objective is to determine whether fewer or smaller quantities of toxic materials can be substituted, making the products safer to manufacture or use. Another company is keeping pace with this new way of thinking: BMW, which is developing a line of automobiles that can be disassembled, and the parts recycled.

Our advice is to determine where you can make the most significant change, then make sure that it is achievable and that consumers will be able to respond to it with their current level of knowledge. Your product research can also be modular: do a certain amount now, then make another leap forward when, for example, a product component is widely available or when the demand for specific cleaning properties (such as "whiter than white") declines or when a waste-disposal option becomes commonplace. This kind of stepped approach to product greening can be seen in the move away from disposable diapers. Originally these diapers were made of bleached pulp. Now they are manufactured using unbleached pulp. The next step—already being actively researched—is to develop a diaper that is fully recyclable rather than disposable.

When you are ready to produce and test a prototype, it will be critical to invest in the best testing methods available. Some companies choose to do extensive consumer market research trials. Procter & Gamble, for instance, launched their product refill containers in a controlled test in Washington, D.C., in November 1989. The product chosen for the test was Downy fabric softener, and the refill packages enabled consumers to both reuse their existing plastic bottles and reduce the amount of packaging they threw out. A similar product, called enviro-pak, was released in Canada at approximately the same time. The success of this unusual green product-and-package in both countries encouraged P&G to make a nationwide launch and to expand the package's contents to include cleaning and personal hygiene products.

Ideas for developing green products may come from unusual places. As we mentioned earlier, consumers are beginning to link health and environmental issues, and demand green products for their larders and medicine chests as well. An interesting new industry has sprung up to meet this growing market segment, and the Harvard University-affiliated environmental group Cultural Survival is its best-known proponent. As we discussed in Chapter Two, Cultural Survival works to promote the rights of indigenous peoples. One of the more creative ways it does this is to import the products of endangered habitats—such as rainforests—to industrial nations, for use in foods and cosmetics. In 1990, for example, Dare Foods Limited added a new product to its line of baked goods, called "Harvest from the Rain Forest."

These cookies are made with brazil nuts from the Amazon rainforest and cashew nuts grown on trees in reforested Amazon areas. The company promotes the item by saying that "buying these cookies helps save the rain forest and the indigenous people who live in it." Other companies, including The Body Shop, are selling fruits, nuts, latex, fish and oils from the rainforest and other threatened areas. Jason Clay, research director of Cultural Survival says that, "We want to show that a living rainforest makes more money than a dead rainforest." Products like this will be very popular with consumers in the 1990s.

We are still a long way from products that are 100 percent green, which means the potential is still enormous. Greening the product is at the Wright brothers stage, and new possibilities and directions open up every month.

While focusing on a single element in product development will work in the short term, in the longer term it won't suffice. Every company that has started to develop green products is becoming familiar with the idea of "cradle-to-grave" assessments of the product, even if this is not yet standard procedure. Staying fixated on a single greener solution may well result in us failing to see an imbalance that created the environmental problem in the first place. This new way of thinking will become more prevalent as the greening of products is improved upon throughout the 1990s, when, for example, appliances and automobiles will include elements that can be repaired, replaced or recycled.

Greening the Package

Loblaws' experience with their "President's Choice" and "No Name" lines told the company that a product's package was an integral part of its success, and it knew that it would be the same with the G.R.E.E.N line. What it didn't know was that the package would have to be much more than just an attractive container.

"The phrase 'walking on eggs' took on new meaning for our company when we tried to introduce the most environmentally friendly egg carton we could design," Patrick recounts. "At that time, we were selling eggs in polystyrene containers. An environmental group told us that the use of CFCs in polystyrene production contributed to ozone depletion and that a switch to CFC-free foam would be greener. Another environmental group informed us that polystyrene, which is very lightweight, was uneconomical to either dispose of or to recycle. So then we discussed pulp cartons, and another environmental group blasted us for our support of an industry that emitted dioxins and furans, and polluted our waterways. When I explained our dilemma to a leading environmentalist I joked that, 'When a customer comes through Loblaws' doors for eggs, we should hand them a chicken.' She smiled knowingly and said, 'May I suggest it be an organic chicken?'"

Packaging, as Loblaws discovered, is big news, and is often singled out as an environmental villain, largely because it is so visible. Various North American surveys have asked consumers what kinds of packaging they think is environmentally harmful. One, conducted by the Council on Plastics and Packaging in the Environment in cooperation with Environmental Research Associates in November 1990, lists consumer preferences as follows: 42 percent of North Americans think plastic is the most environmentally harmful, followed by 14 percent who name metal, 11 percent for aerosol cans, 10 percent who blame excessive packaging in general, 10 percent for paper, 5 percent for polystyrene and 2 percent for glass.

Loblaws had to decide how to protect the product, advertise its features, comply with regulations for sanitation and tamper proofing, meet labeling standards and make the product stand out from the competition, all the while being as environmentally friendly as possible. The company knew it had to tread carefully, due to high public concern about the issue and the way environmental information kept shifting. It relied on the advice of its packaging experts and Pollution Probe to develop packaging for the G.R.E.E.N line. Where possible, that packaging was recyclable or made from recycled materials (such as paper and glass), reusable or manufactured using less raw material (such as lightweight plastics or aluminum, where these were the best alternative).

Packaging professionals are discovering that the environment is taking up increasing amounts of their time, and since the late 1980s, the solid waste issue has overshadowed all other packaging issues combined. "We've got a major environmental issue confronting us," says Gary Fread, vice-president and chief technical officer, Campbell Soup Company Limited, "and it's waste handling. We've got to get on with solving it, and putting it off isn't going to help anyone." Packaging industry associations have begun to develop standards, and are trying to determine what kinds of packages are the most desirable to develop and use. You will need to keep on the leading edge of the ongoing developments in this area. The best strategy is to try to design packaging for five years down the road, rather than what will just squeak by today; you can do this by conferring with environmental groups and listening to what the greenest people in your industry are saying.

Canada's National Packaging Protocol Task Force announced its code of Preferred Canadian Packaging Practices in March 1990. The Code gives preference to systems that use no packaging, followed by those that use minimal packaging, reusable packaging or packaging that contains recycled materials. In the United States a bill is being considered by the state legislatures of Rhode Island, Pennsylvania, Vermont, Maine and Connecticut that would require, over a four-year period, the elimination of toxic metals from most packaging. If passed, it will soon be duplicated in other states. More than anything, however, the message that it is being heard loud and clear is that consumers want "less packaging" and that they want disposal options too.

But there are no clear rights and wrongs in the development of packaging which incorporates sound environmental design. Take the McDonald's polystyrene clamshell as an example. In

December 1990, the company announced it was switching to paper. Some environmentalists believe that the company should have stayed with the clamshell, despite its problems and the public complaints, because polystyrene can be recycled. But the Environmental Defense Fund insists that the scientific data comes down in favor of paper, chiefly because of the 90 percent reduction in volume: polystyrene takes up more space throughout its life, from the time it leaves the factory until the time it ends up in a landfill. "Take a standard McDonald's tractor-trailer," says EDF spokesman Peter Cleary. "It can hold 5,000 clamshells or 50,000 paper wrappers. It's better for the environment to switch to paper—it takes less energy to transport it—and it makes better economic sense for the company too."

As in the case of any kind of packaging, there must be adequate supplies of raw material to create green packaging. A constant supply and level of quality are particularly important for recycled containers, but in the past it has often been difficult to get enough of the recycled product necessary to meet production requirements. When Procter & Gamble worked with its packaging suppliers in the development of recycled paperboard and plastic, it also set to work with local communities so that supply would continue. Product integrity had to be ensured as well. "The inclusion of post-consumer recycled plastic into new bottles could not be accomplished without a major effort by our technical experts," says Doug Moeser, P&G Canada's director of product development, "The process required that bottle strength and visual shelf appearance be maintained, and that the product contents be protected, for example, from odor contamination." The company is also labeling its bottles with plastic-type codes, to assist recyclers in the sorting process.

In sum, if you intend to use recycled materials in your package, your company will have to work with its customers and its suppliers to ensure that your production needs are met. We expect that this will be a growth industry in the next decade. Our conviction is borne out by an A.D. Little survey that indicates that the recycled packaging market will exceed US$500 million by 1995.

Other new types of packaging are under development today, and most are the result of the kind of "green filter" approach we keep referring to. Exciting new developments can be as simple as switching from using cardboard trays to a strip of plastic tape to transport tins of pop from the plant to the retailer. One soda manufacturer made this small change and saved more than US$280,000 in one year alone—and reduced the amount of waste going to the landfill. Other new types of packaging under development include:

- three-layer plastic: a layer of recycled material sandwiched between two layers of virgin material
- shipping merchandise in popcorn, instead of foam chips
- cartons that can be reused, instead of disposed of
- two-part containers, where each element (cardboard and plastic, for example) can be recycled
- water-based (versus chemical- or oil-based) adhesives, and vegetable-based inks and coatings
- labeling systems for plastics and glass so that they can be collected, sorted and recycled (and so that certain types of packaging intended, for example, for pharmaceutical products only can be limited to that product line only)
- the re-emergence of cellophane made from a renewable resource: wood pulp or cotton
- jute-based papers, as an alternative to wood-based products

Microwave packaging warrants a special mention because it has been the target of intense controversy. Its multi-material construction (layers of paper, plastic and foil) makes it difficult to recycle, and the very nature of microwavable foods (often single-serving, convenience-type) has generated controversy. Packaging manufacturers are working to reduce the complexity of the raw materials in each package, and to remove any elements, such as mercury, lead or arsenic (found in labeling) that make it unsafe for landfilling or waste-to-energy disposal. Research into the development of glass microwave packages that would act as cooking devices is now underway; packagers say this new product would also be recyclable.

Material selection and packaging design can have a significant impact on the volume of post-consumer waste, and it is in these two areas that we believe packagers should concentrate their efforts. Another tip is to devise packaging that will be appropriate in the years to come or that can be easily modified to meet rising standards. For example, plastic packaging that is currently made with 25 percent post-consumer plastics can be easily reformulated to include a higher percentage of recycled material when the market demands it, or when supply is readily available.

Food marketers are watching a recent annoucement with great interest. In early 1991 Coke and Pepsi unveiled plans to launch recycled plastic bottles; their design is currently in the approval process with the U.S. Food and Drug Administration. When this bottle is launched, it will be the first time a recycled container has been used for food. "One of the biggest drawbacks to using recycled plastic in food containers," says Melinda Sweet, director of environmental affairs for Unilever subsidiary Lever Brothers, "is the possibility of food contaminating the plastic to be reused. Unilever is really interested in the Coke and Pepsi announcements because of all our food affiliates. Just think of all those margarine containers."

Because what you put on your package is almost as important as what goes into it, we devote a section of "Green Marketing" in the next chapter to a discussion of labeling concerns.

Although a product can be called green if it is marginally greener than the competition's, putting your research and development dollars into the least green alternative you can think of is a poor investment. Increasingly the pioneers are looking at a product's greenness over its entire life cycle. This means finding ways to reduce the harmful impact of a product at every stage of its life from its extraction as a resource through its manufacture, packaging, transportation, consumer use and ultimate disposal (or recycling).

As with all other areas of greening, you cannot rest on your green-product laurels at any stage. You will need to keep reassessing the marketplace, consumer preferences and packaging developments. Loblaws, for example, introduces new additions to its G.R.E.E.N line on a regular basis—recent ones include a peroxide-based alternative to household bleach. And make sure you know your suppliers are living up to their end of the bargain. Ensure that the tuna is not being caught in driftnets, that the paper is made from post-consumer content or that the wood does not come from protected forests.

Developing greener products and greener packages is more complex than traditional product development, where it was once possible to concentrate narrowly on how a product performed and how attractively it was packaged, while keeping an eye on the marketplace for new trends. Soon, no part of a green product's life will be invisible, and green product developers will have to constantly ask how each product fits at every stage into the complex interaction of environmental cause and effect.

Having done your research and developed a product that clearly outgreens the competition, your job in fact has just begun. Successfully marketing a new green product is a separate art, with a whole new set of challenges. For example, you may suddenly find yourself the target of all sorts of abuse. And not just from environmentalists who think you haven't gone far enough. The most damaging backlash may come from one of your own competitors, a company you blithely dismissed as a dinosaur who wasn't doing anything about going green. In fact, the dinosaur was busy figuring out how to launch a counter-attack on your product. We will talk more about this kind of competitor counter-attack response (and the backlash from consumers and environmentalists) in the next chapter. It may not happen, but you had better be prepared just in case.

The green marketplace is a constantly moving target, and you need to adjust your aim continually. Your product's—and your company's—future depend on it.

□ SIX □

Go Public

You have now joined an extremely select group of companies. As of January 1991, we estimate that there were no more than one hundred North American businesses that had committed themselves to going green. These were mostly large corporations, but increasingly they are being joined by medium- and smaller-sized organizations. You have reached this stage because, unlike many of your competitors, you have recognized that concern for the environment is not a passing fad, but one of the major economic forces of this decade and the next.

As one of the "Green 100" you have a lot to tell the world, particularly if you have made genuine progress in cleaning up your own act. And the way you go public with your environmental commitment and accomplishments is as important as any of the steps that have brought you to this point. In fact, it may be more important, since the public reaction to your greening will have a significant impact on your company's future products and profitability. As you publicize your corporate greenness and launch your green products, there will be some major obstacles to hurdle. Not the least of these is the public's natural suspicion of business and its motives. Don't expect the public to cheer you on without reserve. After all, in its eyes you and your colleagues have been destroying the planet since the days of the Industrial Revolution. Patrick often confronts this negative attitude when he is speaking to nonbusiness groups. His reply is straightforward: "We are not stupid people in business, but I will admit that we have been ignorant as to the relationship between economic growth and environmental stewardship. Fortunately that's changing, if for no other reason than that we realize that by continuing to ignore this relationship we will put ourselves out of business." However, we believe—and this is backed up by the experience of a number of green pioneers— that, properly managed, "going public" will ultimately convert even your harshest critics.

There are two major aspects to going public. One is to inform your shareholders, staff and the general public of the actions your company is taking to make itself a more environmentally responsible citizen. The other is to market your newly greened products and services. Of course, each can have a positive spillover effect onto the other, and this cross-fertilization is worth cultivating. In practice, however, many companies have launched their green products before they have finished their internal clean-up. If you do so, be prepared to have to cope with some embarrassing questions—and have your answers ready.

We have already talked about the numerous internal benefits that will come your way as a result of quietly cleaning up your act. Properly handled, going public will reap additional rewards:

1. The public will view your company more favorably and consumers will be more likely to buy all of your products.
2. Environmentalists will give you an easier ride if there is real evidence that your greening is more than skin deep—and they may even become your allies when your anti-green competitors fight back.

3. You will attract more investment in your company.

This last point is a long-term advantage that many businesses overlook. More and more, socially responsible investors are searching for companies with clean environmental records. The most powerful of these investors are the growing number of ethical investment funds and mainstream funds that are making investment decisions based on ethical criteria. Religious institutions such as Canada's Task Force on the Churches and Corporate Responsibility and the American Inter-faith Center for Corporate Responsibility are pressuring mainstream fund managers to invest ethically. In North America, ethical investors control assets worth nearly US$500 billion. Merrill Lynch's extraordinarily successful Environmental Technology Trust is an example of the growing importance of such funds to investors. More than US$128 million was invested in the first two weeks after its launch in the autumn of 1989. The strength of these green funds is such that they are actually forcing changes in corporate behavior. Exxon, for example, bowed to pressure from the New York City employee pension fund which has assets of $30 billion, and put an environmentalist on its board of directors.

This phenomenon is part of a larger trend toward shareholder activism, which in turn is part of a move toward greater public accountability of publicly owned companies. Twenty-four U.S. states have enacted corporate statutes that require directors to consider constituencies other than shareholders—such as employees, suppliers, customers and the community where the company operates. When you go public you are attempting to influence all these constituencies. If you genuinely have something to publicize and you do the job well, you will shape a more positive public perception of your company.

All of this means that public affairs and marketing personnel have to learn a whole new language and acquire a new sensibility. Environmental awareness is becoming a basic operating principle of both corporate public relations and product advertising. The public, and most importantly your customers, are understandably confused about which companies and products are greenest. The people who communicate on your behalf must develop much more sensitivity to environmental concerns, in much the same way as there has been a change in the portrayal of women in advertising. It will be surprisingly easy to make gaffes—like using the metaphor "killing two birds with one stone" in the wrong context. We know of an occasion when these words were innocently uttered at a public forum on corporate environmental responsibility and drew hisses from an aware audience. Until thinking greenly comes more naturally, you will need to watch your every move and edit everything you plan to say.

This chapter takes you through the ABCs of greening your corporate image and introducing your green products to the marketplace.

Write Your Green Mission Statement

Before you step into the media spotlight, one important task remains: the development of your green corporate mission statement. This is a public declaration of your company's environmental commitment that sends a signal that you are serious to constituencies ranging from environmental activists to investors. Your commitment to corporate greening began with the development of your green business strategy. As you moved through each of the stages we suggest in this book, you have been gathering more information that maps out the road to your firm's environmental future. The writing of a corporate mission statement allows you to list each of the elements that you consider crucial to the viability of your business in a sustainable economic framework. The statement can be as simple as a few paragraphs or as detailed as Alcan Aluminum's corporate values statement, which encompasses everything from environmental assessments for new investments and acquisitions to waste-minimization objectives. Alberta's TransAlta Utilities Corporation, an environmental leader among

North American electric utilities, has recently released an Environmental Policy Statement that is a model of what a mission statement should be:

> TransAlta is committed to the protection of the environment and to sustainable development. Environmental stewardship is a vital element in our business. We strive to empower all our employees to take initiatives to protect and enhance the environment, based on shared values and the need to satisfy the environmental concerns and expectations of customers, investors and the public. Our commitments are to:
>
> - report complete and accurate information on the environmental impact of our business, meet or surpass all environmental standards, and continuously improve our environmental performance
> - advocate socially responsible environmental standards and the recognition of the economic value of environmental resources
> - implement conservation and efficiency initiatives for all resources and pursue alternative energy opportunities, both within our own operations and in partnership with others
> - seek out research opportunities and develop alliances that will improve our environmental performance and make a positive contribution to solving environmental challenges
> - consult and work co-operatively with those who may be affected by our business and respond to their environmental concerns
> - recognize and respect the relationship between environment and health in all phases of our business, and use the best knowledge available to protect the health of employees and the public
> - encourage the development of educational programs and resources, to provide balanced public information

and to foster environmentally sensitive attitudes, knowledge and skills

- identify and develop business ventures where value can be added to environmental solutions while providing investment opportunities for the corporation and its shareholders.

TransAlta's environmental mission statement incorporates each of the elements identified by green corporate pioneers: the tracking and logging of information on operations, the effective management of resources and energy and the development of alliances with others. It recognizes the inherent soundness of the concept of sustainable development, makes a commitment to working toward it and states the intention to communicate all of the above to the public. And it makes its points in a modest, conservative way, which helps convey the company's basic sincerity and trustworthiness. Our recommendation is that your own environmental mission statement include these important ideas, and that they then become an integral part of your green business strategy.

Publicize Your Newly Green Company

Your most recent environmental audit told you exactly what you have to communicate. Your ongoing dialogue, and possible alliance, with environmental groups means that you are more prepared and confident about current environmental concerns and that you have a reasonable notion of what the next green "wave" will be. Your vice-president of environmental affairs has been honing your corporate message and refining strategy for this decade. In other words, you now have a great deal of positive information about your company. So how do you communicate this good news to the public with maximum impact? Obviously every company and situation is different, but certain lessons can be learned from those who have already been through the process. Although this section concentrates on corporate publicity, much of the advice is applicable to marketing green products and services, a subject we deal with in the second half of this chapter.

In 1990 AT&T ran a national print ad in publications such as *Business Week* that was headlined "Most Nightmares Disappear When You Wake Up." The densely worded ad revolved around the decision of Pittsburgh residents to clean up their city, reversing the damage to their atmosphere and environs. The basic message was that "working together, we can and must make this earth a better place to live." The punchline was that, as a company, AT&T was doing just that in thirty-seven countries around the world: cutting chlorofluorocarbon use, recycling, eliminating environmental hazards at source so that "someday very soon, we can all wake up in a better place." This effective ad communicated (1) the company's acknowledgment of the importance of environmental issues, (2) the need to work together toward a stated goal and (3) what AT&T was doing as a company. It was head and shoulders above most of the ads other companies were running. This next section we will outline how you can follow their excellent lead.

Plan Your Strategy

Publicizing your company's greenness may be an even more delicate proposition than marketing new green products. No matter how thorough your internal clean-up has been, it is very likely you have missed something. Cleaning up your act is an ongoing process and what was environmentally okay last week may be a problem this week. Whatever you say and whatever media you choose to say it in, your message will be carefully scrutinized by environmentalists, truth-in-advertising lobbies and possibly regulators.

The best strategy of all is to make sure that what you plan to say is true, and also credible. Inaccurate or erroneous information will pull the green rug out from under you. In the United

Kingdom, media are turning away green advertisers whose campaigns could be construed as being inaccurate. This will soon happen in North America. We highly recommend backing up your claims with documentation (which will also prepare you to counter the backlash we talk about later in this chapter). Going public is your chance to make people understand your position and to win their support. It is your opportunity to say clearly that you have taken note of their environmental concerns and that this is what you are doing about the issues. You are only going to be able to do this by developing a campaign that is believable and appropriate for the subject matter.

AT&T's ad was successful because it was very direct about the fact that there are problems, it acknowledged that the company—like so many others—contributes to these problems and it described what the company was doing to reverse this polluting trend. And, as with TransAlta's low-key mission statement, AT&T's ad works because it doesn't turn the environment into a mushy motherhood statement like "We know you care about the planet and we want you to know that we care too." Far too many companies are still resorting to this sort of vague emotional appeal. By contrast, AT&T's ad is based on some stated truths and will go a long way, we believe, to ensure public support of future AT&T ad campaigns. Be candid. If you have only recently begun your corporate greening but your commitment is genuine, say so. Your environmental intelligence gathering has revealed which issues are most relevant to your company and of most concern to the public. Stay with what you know your audience will understand. Educate them gradually. Be forthright about your company's goals and objectives.

Who you want to talk to and what they want to hear will help determine what you say. Who will your campaign target: the general public? environmental groups? investors? the media? This is your chance to help set the record straight about your environmental performance and how you perceive your firm's role in the overall trend toward corporate greening.

Next, determine exactly what you want to say. Decide at the outset whether you want to talk about the general environment-friendliness of your company, or perhaps zero in on a specific green innovation that has moved you ahead of regulations or your competitors. Ask yourself what sets your company apart. Apart from what you would traditionally publicize—product quality, excellence of service, strength of management—focus clearly on how your environmental performance or general environmental commitment can be promoted.

Now decide what form your campaign should take. Should you advertise or launch a public relations plan—or both? While you may have relied exclusively on corporate image campaigns in the past—primarily television and print advertising—these are no longer enough. Communications industry experts agree that going public with your corporate and product greenness is different and requires a more direct approach. This means diversifying your campaign to include a public relations component, so that editorial coverage is generated (more than anywhere else the credibility that comes from news coverage or a mention in a widely read column can have a larger and longer-lasting impact than advertisements). People are more inclined to believe your message when it comes from a reporter than when it appears in an ad. You already know that opinion leaders can make or break you—and with green, in the midst of high skepticism about corporate motives, this is even more crucial.

Finally, begin to plan your campaign in detail, working with in-house marketing and public affairs staff as well as your advertising agency. (We recommend that your public affairs department be a part of the team from the earliest stages of your corporate greening. This way, it will be able to prepare a strategy that has real substance and be able to make specific recommendations throughout the process, as opportunities to go public arise.) The remainder of this section examines the different forms that publicizing your newly green company can take, and illustrates some of the more successful approaches others have adopted.

One final word of advice here: although it may seem obvious, it is crucial that your in-house team and your ad agency are conversant with environmental issues and the current level of public awareness of these issues. You must have this research in hand before you develop your campaign, and we recommend that you vet any of your more powerful claims with someone who is an environmental expert. Just as companies acting with the best of intentions created some products we class as false starts, well-meaning firms have also launched some highly inaccurate public campaigns. This kind of blunder will set you back considerably.

Working with the Media

Your green corporate campaign's diversified approach should include extensive liaison with the media. As we said above, favorable press coverage is generally the best way to reach opinion leaders, and your message will likely enjoy maximum credibility as editorial copy rather than advertising.

Make the development of media contacts a priority. Not only is publicity more labor-intensive than advertising, but the number of potential contacts is multiplying every quarter. Media giants are hiring environmental reporters as quickly as the corporate community is bringing in vice-presidents of the environment. It seems as if every publication deals with the environment these days, and even the biggest names in hard news and business coverage are writing green cover stories. In the United States, *Business Week* has given the environment extensive and in-depth coverage, with *Fortune*, *Time* and *Newsweek* running a close second. *The Los Angeles Times*, *New York Times* and *Wall Street Journal* have environmental reporters on their business desks who write top-notch articles. In Canada, several publications are developing excellent reputations for their coverage of the environment. For example, *The Financial Post* not only covers breaking environmental stories with a business angle, but includes regular columns on different aspects of green business—

legal and insurance concerns, for example. Canadian-based *New Environment Magazine* is the newest addition to the North American media roster. Designed as a forum for information exchange on environmental issues, its regular features include green economics, marketing, financing, law, consumers and media. England's *The Economist* is already widely read by business; we recommend their environmental coverage highly. In addition, publications that target specific groups of readers, such as *Advertising Age*, *Marketing*, *Institutional Investor* and *Management Review* regularly cover environmental issues.

The same holds true for electronic media: radio and television newscasts now frequently feature environmental stories. In the United States, Cable News Network stands head and shoulders above other television networks in its coverage of the environment. Ted Turner, CEO and chairman of Turner Broadcasting, has even released a publication called *Ten Voluntary Initiatives for Environmental Action.*

Whether it is in the form of documentaries, features, profiles or news coverage, everyone is looking to produce, read, watch or listen to environmental stories. And each of these media outlets' environmental commentators needs a constant supply of good story ideas, which is where your company comes in. As you have brought your staff on side and cleaned up your operations, there is a good chance many good green stories have come to light. Your public relations staff should by now have a large file of these anecdotes, which can now be fed to the appropriate media. The best stories are those with strong human interest, for example, a staff person's idea that turned out to be a green goldmine, or a dramatic environmental improvement, such as the fact that you've switched from a toxic cleanser to soap and water.

Redken Laboratories, a leading U.S. hair care company, was able to generate press for one of its innovative ideas by piggybacking on a breaking news story. When Redken's vice-president of research, Dr. Lee Hunter, heard news reports of what was happening to sea mammals caught in the Alaskan oil spill, he moved quickly. "The scientists in Alaska took immediate action to clean the oil off the sea otters," Dr. Hunter says. "But there was not a procedure to 'condition' the fur and skin, which had to replenish the natural oils in their skins, which is necessary to save their lives." Dr. Hunter and staff worked with the company's existing hair conditioners and found a way to treat the otters' skin after cleaning. The company's genuine good deed saved more than eighty sea otters and generated lots of press; the media are always looking for a new angle on a story they have to cover over an extended period.

Don't just know your media, get to know the reporters. You will be most successful at placing a story if you know exactly where the release should go. Hire public relations people who know the field and can get to know the issues, as well as who in your company is responsible for which aspect of your operations. In 1990 a group of U.S. environmental reporters founded the Society of Environmental Journalists. The association's newsletter is an excellent source of such writers, and its "Green Belt" section lists story ideas, reviews outstanding coverage and lists media that have just added an environmental journalism beat.

"Sometimes the reporters will get to know you," says Patrick. "We were amused when, in August 1990, *Toronto Life* magazine did a cover story on the Blue Boxes of our city's 'rich and famous', which detailed the curbside recycling habits of some of the city's leading citizens. Naturally, Loblaw International Merchants President David Nichol was one of the chosen few; his box's contents passed with flying colors."

Now that you have surveyed the field there are some important pointers to keep in mind when dealing with the media on the subject of your green story:

1. *Define your company's story.* Know what you want to talk about, and organize your information clearly; look for angles (or "hooks" as they are known in the trade); remember that anecdotes can add color to an otherwise dry profile; review the important facts that you are likely to be asked about; keep

in mind that real news has a much better chance of generating coverage. An initiative like the McDonald's decision to switch from polysytrene to paper will get covered from coast to coast but a news release on your thirty-second type of recycled paper will go straight to the local landfill. And be ready to piggy-back your company on a breaking news item, but only use this tactic when your contribution is significant, as in the Redken example.

2. *Define the environmental issues that are likely to be linked to your company,* and face them head on. Candidness is the most effective strategy for dealing with the media. More than ever before, an open door policy is expected of the greenest companies, and your coverage is likely to be more favorable if you don't shy away from the more difficult issues. "No comment" is no longer good enough. If there is a problem, for example, with toxic chemicals at one of your plants and you want to go public with the environmental initiatives at head office, state the facts, and discuss what your plans are to remedy the situation. Misrepresenting the facts to the media can do long-term damage from which it will be difficult to recover.

3. Once an interview has been arranged, or if you are approached by a reporter, make sure that you *organize your information in advance.* Feel free to ask what general topics will be covered, but don't demand a list of questions (this is a red flag that often tells a journalist you've got something to hide). During the interview, remember three things: everything you say is on the record; mistakes are correctable (just say, "No, that's wrong, what I meant to say was ... " and correct yourself); relax—answers that are not rehearsed sound much more natural and believable. You know all about your company's greening, your mission statement and your products, so just prepare yourself and then tell it like it is.

Once the story has run, or if a piece appears in the media that you didn't contribute to, and there are blatant inaccuracies, you are well within your rights to correct them by contacting the writer. If this is done with good intentions and in a rational manner, most journalists will want to hear your side. Don't forget that environmental-business issues are as new to many reporters as they are to your company, so they will probably appreciate your attempt to set the record straight. (Do not go over the journalist's head unless you feel there has been a serious misrepresentation of the facts, and you're getting nowhere with the writer.)

Keep these ideas in mind when you are trying to manage a crisis situation such as a toxic chemical spill and when responding to a counter-attack. Don't overreact and become defensive. This will only generate more interest, as the natural supposition will be that you have something to cover up. Make yourself available for interviews, provide updated information at regular intervals, and you will come out of the crisis with your reputation intact—or at the very least, you won't do your company any more harm.

One final bit of advice: make sure that your company's products and services are included in green consumer guides—particularly now that you are confident they will get favorable reviews.

Techniques for Going Public

In this section we look at some of the most effective ways of communicating your good deeds to the public.

Press Conference

A press conference provides an opportunity for you to reveal an important development to an assembled group of journalists, other than the few key media representatives with whom you have been working hard to establish a good relationship. We caution you to choose this communication vehicle only when your company has something very important to talk about— otherwise your next press conference will be deserted. Your goal is to announce some specific new information at a specified time. The same ideas we reviewed in "working with the media" apply here: have your information organized, know the facts, be honest and open and be prepared to answer all questions.

Choose this option when your company has just made a sizable financial commitment to improve its environmental record, when you are launching a foundation that will support nonprofit community environmental actions, when you are announcing an important merger or acquisition that has unusual environmental components or when ground-breaking technology is being released to the marketplace. Your public affairs people will be able to organize this event, book the space—generally a local public place, such as a hotel—invite key media, ensure that your company's top personnel (those with appropriate knowledge of the issues involved) are present, and prepare pertinent factual information on your corporate announcement and general background information about your company for distribution at the press conference.

Don't forget to give your press conference a visual component. It's a good idea to have charts, photographs, video, product and anything else you think will appeal to both a television audience and news photographers. Plan to include some action, such as two CEOs shaking hands, or a demonstration of your new green product.

One final note. Media launches, as opposed to press conferences, are generally reserved for products, rather than corporate announcements. We will talk more about this technique in the "Green Marketing" section of this chapter.

Public Events

There will be times when you want to involve more than the media in launching your green publicity campaign. Communities want to know that local companies are cleaning up their acts, and there are numerous ways to initiate events that allow you to publicize some good green news or your overall environmental commitment. This is also an excellent opportunity to go public with your environmental mission statement. (Monsanto prints its statement on cards and hands them out at all community events.

You can't get your message across more directly than this.)

The range of public events in which companies are involved is wide: from cleaning up local roadways to tree plantings in local neighborhoods, to participating in community-based environmental events and conferences. We believe that public events are an excellent way to discover your community's main environmental concerns and what local people think of your company, and also an excellent way to get your staff involved in the greening of your organization. It is difficult for people to remain cynical about your intentions when they see top brass and line staff sweating over spadefuls of earth while planting trees along a previously barren roadway.

A public event doesn't have to be in your backyard. Huntsman Chemical Corp. and Dow Chemical Company are the hosts of a joint recycling program that has been established in a number of U.S. national parks. Tourists in Great Smokey Mountains National Park in North Carolina, Grand Canyon in Arizona and Acadia in Maine helped the companies kick off the program in June 1990 by cleaning up picnic areas and roadways throughout the parks. When the program is fully operational, garbage will be cut by 25 percent.

Local communities will have an increasingly important impact on operations. It is smart policy to build bridges today.

Annual Meetings/Annual Reports

Your annual general meeting and the publication of your annual report are excellent opportunities to go public with your environmental mission statement. They are also good occasions to report on your environmental performance and intentions to shareholders, investors and media. Loblaw Companies Limited's annual report for 1989 included an insert about the company's G.R.E.E.N program. The special section, printed on recycled paper, described how the line got started, what range of products it includes and why the company ventured into the green arena, then recapped the success of the products.

But don't go overboard with your environmental message at the meeting or in your annual report. A handful of the executives we spoke with said that there was grumbling from media—and some shareholders—when the overriding focus of an AGM was green. Although an environmental theme for your annual report may work occasionally, green is not the only thing your constituents are interested in hearing about.

Your annual meeting can be an excellent opportunity to communicate exactly why your company is committed to greening and what the benefits will be. There will inevitably be some shareholders in the audience who think you are spending too much on environmental initiatives, so be prepared for their tough questions. Although in many cases it is difficult to isolate the portion of your profits that are green, this is sometimes possible. For example, 3M keeps a running tab of the revenue generated by its Pollution Prevention Pays program in its annual reports.

Report Cards

This new technique takes a page from your critic's book. For years concerned citizen groups have published "report cards" on a company's environmental performance, rating its operations and overall performance. More recently, companies in the resource sector have begun to file their own report cards. They believe that self-disclosure is an effective way to control the flow of information about what goes on behind plant gates. Writing your own report card is a superb way to disarm your critics and underline the seriousness of your commitment to greening.

The Monsanto Chemical Company began issuing "performance report cards" in 1988 and continues to do so on a regular basis. The company refers to these public notices as "Backgrounders." These usually include a review of the goals that were previously set, make reference to appropriate legislation and highlight the company's success in meeting its obligations. The "Backgrounders" are distributed widely—to the media, local resident's groups, regulators and environmentalists.

Dow Chemical Canada Inc. released its first twelve-page environmental report card in the summer of 1989. Hailed by many as a "challenging standard," the report detailed Dow's 1988–89 operations, described Dow's objectives and reported results on more than sixty environment-related projects. The report trumpeted the company's successes, but it also did something very unusual: it pointed a finger at a serious unsolved environmental problem, in this case, the discharging of eight kilograms of highly toxic waste into the St. Clair River every day from Dow's Sarnia, Ontario division. The company says the report is part of its commitment to an open-door policy, and the community clearly agrees with the move: with each subsequent edition, the number of requests for copies increased substantially.

Publications

In addition to your annual report, all of your existing communication vehicles should be used to carry your message to your target audience. The list of people you want to communicate with in this way include staff, customers, suppliers, competitors, regulators, press and investors.

Use your newsletters, staff newspapers, bulletin boards and in-house video programming to spread the word about what you're doing. You can publish special editions of these, as did both AT&T and Noranda. Or you can include a regular column in an existing publication, so that people can turn to it for the latest information and ideas, as Bell Canada chose to do with its staff newsletter.

Make use of the communications network your public relations and human resources people have already established. This section of your "community"—your employees—wants to know what the company's plans are, what new products have been launched, what kind of return there is on green investment and whether the ideas they have been suggesting are being used.

Green Corporate Advertising

Advertising is a powerful way to create a lasting public perception of your company's environmental practices. While in the past you may have relied heavily on advertising—perhaps even to the exclusion of other communications strategies, it should not be the only element you use in promoting your corporate greenness. In fact, in many cases it may even be wise to ignore advertising completely.

There are, however, occasions when you can make green ads pay. McDonald's had been under attack for years for its contribution to the solid waste problem when it launched a successful ad in April 1990. Newspapers across North America carried a one-page ad announcing the company's McRecycle USA program, a commitment to buy at least US$100 million worth of building and remodeling products made with recycled materials. The ads included an 800 number for suppliers to call, and most observers say that the ads (and the program) were an effective way for McDonald's to communicate what it is doing to improve its environmental image.

As with all green publicity, if you do your homework first, your ad campaign will have greater impact. GTE, the telephone company, ran a two-page ad in the Seattle area informing customers where they could take their outdated Yellow Pages for recycling. Thirty percent of the local population responded by doing just that. The ads worked astonishingly well, but only because the company knew that phonebooks were a major disposal problem and had worked out a solution. Before it ran the ad GTE lined up recyclers who would take the books. Thus the ad kept working as long as the phonebooks were being recycled.

Most ad industry professionals agree that a continuous, incremental advertising strategy is very effective for a green message. Don't make huge promises: state your commitment, describe what you are doing now and what you think you can accomplish in the future. The Wal-Mart supermarket chain ran a series of television and print ads with the headline "We're looking for quality products guaranteed not to last" and subtitled, "We're challenging our manufacturing partners to improve their products to help prevent lasting environmental problems." The ad went on to say it would reward compliant suppliers with free in-store advertising. The company's belief that supplying green products for its customers was a first step toward sustainable practices was very effectively portrayed to both suppliers and consumers.

Lever Brothers Company, a soap manufacturing subsidiary of Unilever, took another approach altogether by emphasizing consumer education in a campaign titled "Is your favourite brand packaged for generations to come?" The ad discussed the company's move toward recycled plastics for its product and asked for consumers' help in ensuring an adequate supply. The tag line was "shared world, shared responsibility."

Our general advice for good green ads is this: If you have a solid, technically defensible position, "sell it." But there is one thing that won't sell—in a word, glitz. You are selling much more than the sizzle in the steak when you sell green. "The ad business is prone to clichés and slogans, and that is definitely the wrong way to go," says Allan Beaver, of Levine, Huntley, Schmidt & Beaver Advertising, New York City. "People are suspicious of advertising of any kind. We have to make the environment hit home, especially with the economy being what it is today. People are worried about putting food on the table. We have to make the environment relevant to their lives."

One of the most serious indictments to date of a corporate ad campaign occurred in the United Kingdom when Scott Paper was lambasted for serious inaccuracies in its advertising. Scott's campaign aimed to convince consumers that the company's forestry operations didn't contribute to the greenhouse effect because the company grows trees that store carbon dioxide, therefore helping reduce global warming trends. Environmental Data Services (EDS), a London-based research group pointed out to the media that in its opinion Scott's campaign ignored the fact that its reforestation replaces pre-existing vegetation that already contained carbon. In addition, EDS charged, Scott and its suppliers "burn and use fossil fuels in order to grow, harvest, manufacture and distribute the firm's product." Furthermore, the disposal of the company's major product—paper—is chiefly in landfills, where it degrades and creates methane, another greenhouse gas. EDS concluded that "the likelihood is that the company, far from 'countering' the greenhouse effect, is contributing to it." Whether or not EDS was correct, this public vilification is the sort of thing companies must be prepared for.

Avoid any misinformation or exaggerated claims. Reports of companies promoting cars that don't damage the ozone layer and washing machines that help protect newt-habitats may be amusing, but they also damage the whole green advertising field. And clichés are instant death: Earth Day 1990 was a wonderful opportunity for business to reach a huge audience. But too many organizations took a short cut and ran ads that didn't really say much about what they were doing and did them little good—or even some harm—in the consumer's mind. "Every day is Earth Day" is a prime example of an overused slogan. No fewer than six organizations used it in the spring of 1990.

Advertising in the environmental media is gaining popularity with media directors who want to target the greenest consumers. For example, in 1990, Ogilvy & Mather placed U.S. clothing manufacturer Osh Kosh ads in upscale publications such as *GQ*, but added some surprising new names to the list: *Garbage*, *E Magazine* and *Buzzworm*. All three are environmental publications targeted at consumers, and all had been launched in the previous eighteen months. All kinds of new publications are being read by green consumers. They are appearing so fast that your ad placement strategy needs constant updating.

A new kind of marketing requires new ways of thinking about not only what kind of ad to place but where to place it. Some companies are advertising in provincial and state park guides, and others are printing their message on every truck in their fleet. Motorists on Toronto's Gardiner Expressway drive by an unusual series of ads on their way to and from work each day. In the midst of a sea of billboards, a local entrepreneur designed all-natural advertising for the highway embankments. The ads spell out the advertiser's message in flowers, shrubs and other greenery; to date Minolta, Imperial Oil and The Canadian National Railways have signed up.

Finally, there is one situation when advertising is never the right strategy. That is, when your name has been linked to some environmental bad news. If this happens be straight with the media, but don't run an ad campaign. "Exxon after the Alaskan spill, and Union Carbide after Bhopal are much better off not saying anything than trying to repair the damage done to their company's image through advertising," says Peter A. Greene, President and CEO of Saatchi & Saatchi Canada. "Whatever they said in an ad would lack credibility."

The green revolution will likely see not only new ideas in advertising, but some unexpected advertising partnerships. In a surprising turn of events, Coke and Pepsi are running a joint ad campaign. In 1991, the companies launched a "green generation" campaign that promotes the recyclable bottles. The tag line is "returnable, reusable, remarkable," and the campaign is surely a sign of things to come.

Market Your New Green Products

There is no doubt that environmental awareness is influencing purchasing decisions locally, nationally and globally—and that marketers are moving quickly to adjust to this fact. Even Japan, which lags far behind Europe and North America in most aspects of the green consumer revolution, has recently discovered green marketing. For example, a new Japanese beer produced by Suntory is called "The Earth." The beer is sold in cans and bottles that bear the slogan, "Suntory is thinking about the earth." In fact, the Japanese Advertising Council reports that nature preservation was the most important advertising campaign theme of 1990. Throughout the developed world, the growing success of green products and services is fast propelling green marketing to the forefront of current business activities.

Given the rise of the green consumer and given the fact that many companies are now scrambling to capture their share of this new market, how do you make sure your green product or service will succeed? While the market for such products is potentially quite large and growing rapidly, it is still in the early stages and is not unlimited. To reach that market you must do your homework, which means thorough market research and the development of a product that is truly greener than the competition's, factors we covered in detail in Chapter Five.

The first rule of green marketing is: never forget who the new green consumer is. While he or she may still be a citizen of the consumer society, new ideas are beginning to compete with established consumer values. While convenience and ease of disposal have driven marketing since the Second World War, this will no longer be the case in the emerging green marketplace. In essence, this new consumer is a consumer with a conscience, someone who looks beyond the product or service and considers, however briefly or simplistically, its content, its impact on the earth and the range of alternatives. This consumer is still evolving and green marketers are actively trying to anticipate the next level of green consumer consciousness.

One of the easiest mistakes you can make is to ignore the environmental impact of your green marketing methods. This is a criticism frequently encountered by pollsters. In a 1990 *Marketing News* survey respondents complained about problems ranging from excess packaging and the disposable nature of product samples to the huge volume of direct mail they receive, little of it on recycled paper. Consumers are much less enchanted than they used to be with the idea that they must always have something new—even if it is green; they are more drawn to products that are durable, recyclable or reusable. And though we've said it before, it is worth stressing: shoppers will turn away from any product that makes false green claims for itself and from any company that markets a token green product or two but does nothing else to clean up its act.

"I would advise anybody to take a good look inside their company before they start advertising the environmental aspects of their products," says Russel Wohlwerth, vice-president and supervisor of DDB Needham, a Los Angeles ad agency. "If you are polluting streams that are going to be ruined for the next 10,000 years, it doesn't matter if your box is biodegradable. When people see you contradicting yourself, you come off as a liar, which is a P.R. disaster."

Your experience with bringing other products to the marketplace has shown you that it takes a long time to develop desirable attributes such as trust, respect and service. Environmental marketing illustrates this important point in an even more acute way: you can't buy green brand loyalty, you have to earn it. Properly handled, a green campaign will do your market share a world of good, mismanaged it will do more than destroy a product—it can destroy your company's credibility.

Design an Effective Green Label

Before you go public with your product, you need to design its label. What you put on the package is an extremely important part of your green marketing strategy, because it determines how successfully you distinguish your product from the competition— including the emerging green competition. In October 1990 Princeton-based Environmental Research Associates surveyed one thousand Americans and found that 64 percent looked for green labeling at least part of the time. The most effective green label is one that is immediately recognizable as identifying an environmentally improved product. It should also contain certain facts about the product's environmental benefits. Two questions you should consider are:

1. How do you make your green products instantly recognizable? and
2. How do you list your product's environmental strengths?

As we discussed in Chapter Five, Loblaws' answer to question number one was to create a distinctive corporate brand for its line of green products. To ensure that the name they chose, G.R.E.E.N, wasn't usurped by a competitor, Loblaws immediately applied to have it registered as a trademark (the only way the word green could be trademarked was with periods between each letter).

Next, Loblaws had to decide what information to put on the label. It was clear from the start that each package had to list—in the simplest terms—why this product was better for the environment than another product. It did this by devoting a section of the label exclusively to information about why the product is environmentally improved. Loblaws' G.R.E.E.N 100 percent chlorine-free coffee filters box reads: "Unlike most North American coffee filters which are bleached with environmentally-harmful chlorine, these premium quality filters have never been bleached; their natural creamy-tan colour is an indication of their environment friendly manufacturing process and will not alter the taste of your coffee. Now you can drink coffee while doing something good for the environment." The products endorsed by Pollution Probe were similarly labeled. G.R.E.E.N maxi-pads carried this information, "Endorsed by Pollution Probe because they are made with 100 percent non-chlorine-bleached fluff pulp. Fluff pulp plays an important role in the manufacturing of sanitary napkins. In order to get sanitary napkins white, most fluff pulp in North America is bleached with chlorine-based chemicals which can cause serious, long-term environmental problems. The chlorine bleaching process creates a chemical waste that is washed into rivers and seas where it is harmful to fish and sea life. Fortunately, it is no longer necessary to produce sanitary napkins using chlorine-bleached fluff pulp. The fluff pulp in this product is produced in one of the most technologically advanced mills in North America. It uses a hydrogen peroxide bleaching process that produces oxygen and water as waste products. As a result, water pollution is kept to an absolute minimum. What's more, this revolutionary new pulp technology production uses half the number of trees conventional sanitary napkins require. We feel this is an important step towards saving our natural resources. Unlike the artificial white colour of ordinary, chlorine-bleached pads, the natural creamy colour of this product is an indication of its environmentally friendly manufacturing process. —Pollution Probe."

What information should you put on your green label? The simplest answer is: everything that contributes to the product's environment-friendliness, however insignificant it may seem. Here is a short list of what you might include:

- what the product is made of
- what the package is made of
- how it was made (i.e. that it takes less energy to manufacture)
- its impact on the waste stream (e.g., that it is recyclable)
- any other related information, such as that a percentage of each sale goes to an environmental group

Although much of this may seem obvious, experienced companies have often overlooked the obvious. You may already have many products in the marketplace that can be relabeled to become green. For years a U.S. cereal manufacturer included the line "made from recycled fibers" on its box tops. In the late 1980s, since no one seemed to be paying attention, it removed the reference. The Packaging Institute advised the company to put the line back on, and advises all packagers and manufacturers to promote their greenness in a similar fashion. A 1990 Gallup poll of manufacturers and packagers found that although 50 percent of them have adopted recycled packaging, only one-third listed this information on their package.

Procter & Gamble's new recycled plastic bottles carry neck hangers that read "Now this contains 25 percent recycled plastic." This is a good example of the kind of labeling that works well: it is factual, specific, simple and unambiguous.

Dare's Harvest from the Rain Forest cookie package carries on all four sides information about why this product is environment-friendly, and the bottom panel carries this message, "Questions or comments? Dare would like to hear from you," along with an 800 number. The side panels include an address for Cultural Survival, the advocacy group that helped the company develop the cookies.

What you say on your green label in North America has, until now, been largely up to you. But standards are being quickly developed in response to consumer confusion about green claims, and the industry's own desire to rationalize the meaning of terms such as "recyclable." In the United States a ten-state task force of attorneys general was set up to investigate truth-in-advertising claims for green products. "The National Association of Attorneys General has adopted a resolution," says Task Force head Hubert H. Humphrey III, Attorney General of Minnesota, "to work with the Federal Trade Commission and Environmental Protection Agency to establish a common base of regulation that would help define uniform standards in this area." The task force's proposal suggests that until national standards are developed by the FTC or EPA marketers should follow these voluntary regulations:

- environmental claims should be as specific as possible, not general, vague, incomplete or overly broad—such as "environmentally friendly" and "safe for the environment"
- disposability claims should not be made unless that disposal option is available in the area in which the product is sold
- green claims should be substantive—avoid trivial and irrelevant claims that give a false impression of a product's overall environmental soundness
- environmental claims should be supported by competent and reliable scientific evidence

A final note about labeling. As we discussed in Chapter Two, while eco-labeling—that is, the official certification of goods and services according to green criteria—is still in its infancy in North America, it is doing very well in Germany, and as this book goes to press, the European Community is announcing details of their program. The programs are not without their flaws—the main one being that they are only comparative, selecting "better" rather than "best" products—but they have the unequivocal support of government and consumers. Loblaws has applied for approval for those G.R.E.E.N products that fit into eco-labeling categories under Canada's Environmental Choice program—a sure sign that despite the huge success of its in-house labeling, it believes third-party approval is ultimately the way to go. Earth Island Institute's dolphin-safe rating is an example of how powerful such approvals can be.

Launch Your Green Products and Services

Just as with the rest of your corporate greening, successful environmental marketing begins with a genuine commitment to the environment, and sound strategic planning. This section will highlight the ways that green marketing differs from publicizing your newly green company. The list of factors you need to keep in mind bear repeating: green consumer trends, a knowledge of pertinent green regulations, a solid awareness of key environmental issues and a clear sense of what your competitors are doing.

When you are ready to launch your green products and services, you will need to identify the best vehicles, whether they be in-store promotions, advertising, public relations, a press conference, trade shows or direct mail. If what you have developed is really new and different, attention will be forthcoming. This was certainly true for Loblaws.

The company had developed a very successful television ad approach for its "President's Choice" line, which featured Loblaw International Merchants President David Nichol talking about the particular product they were promoting that month. It used the same technique to promote the launch of G.R.E.E.N, only this time it invited someone to share center stage with Nichol—Colin Isaacs. Nichol encouraged shoppers to change supermarkets so that they could buy green products, which no one else was carrying. Loblaws also used its successful newspaper insert, *The Insider's Report*, to showcase the new line. The report runs a dozen pages on average, and in addition to listing new items and goods on special, it takes the shoppers behind the scenes by explaining the decision-making process that goes into the selection of each product. G.R.E.E.N worked particularly well in this medium because it gave Nichol a chance to expand on Loblaws' reasons for launching the line and to describe the environmental pluses of each product. He also wrote an open letter to Loblaws' customers that ran on the front page of the June 1989 *Insider's*. It read, in part:

Here are a few points of clarification about the program.

1. With few exceptions, President's Choice G.R.E.E.N products are priced at, or below the price of the national brands to which they are an alternative.

2. We do not intend to censor products that some may feel are "environmentally-unfriendly." We see our role as providing a choice so you may decide for yourself.

3. Protecting the environment is a young and therefore imprecise science. As a result, not all groups agree on what the best products are to help control pollution. For example, some advise us to use paper pulp trays for all eggs while others say recyclable, ozone-friendly foam trays made with pentane instead of chlorofluorocarbons (CFCs) are a better solution. We accept the fact that it is inevitable that not all environmental groups will agree with all of our "President's Choice" G.R.E.E.N products.

4. Some may accuse us of being "environmental opportunists." We see our role as providing products that people want. That's why we created "No Name" products when Canada's food inflation was running at 16 percent. That's why we created President's Choice products when a demand for quality products arose. And that's why we've created G.R.E.E.N

products when the overwhelming concern of Canadians is the environment.

We invite you to read about our new President's Choice G.R.E.E.N products in this Insider's Report and decide for yourself whether or not they fill a real need in our society.

5. A number of our G.R.E.E.N products are products that we've carried for years (such as baking soda). Putting them under the G.R.E.E.N label was in response to environmental groups who chided us by saying, "You have a number of products in your stores right now that could help fight pollution but you have to bring them to your customers' attention and then explain how to use them."

Advertising is not the only way to successfully launch a new green product. The Body Shop never advertises, relying instead on press coverage, which it is particularly adept at generating. This is partly because the company's code of ethics and evolving all-natural product line is unusual enough to attract ongoing interest. But it is also partly due to an unusual corporate policy that requires each staff member to give at least two hours per week in community service. As a result, the company has a terrific public profile; word of mouth is one of its best promotional vehicles. As we indicated in the section on corporate self-promotion, developing a good relationship with the community is part of a diversified publicity strategy—and often carries more credibility than other options.

In August of 1990 Procter & Gamble and Du Pont Canada chose a press conference to help them go public with their joint plastic recycling initiative. The companies rented Toronto's SkyDome (a sports stadium) and filled a corner of the field with the number of bottles they estimated would be eliminated from landfills in that year through the program. It was an excellent presentation, and garnered terrific media attention for the two firms.

Companies are taking a wide variety of communications approaches to green marketing. Direct-mail marketers are printing their catalogues on recycled paper. Lever's 100 percent phosphate-free Sunlight detergent ads broke new ground by being the first to promote the greenness of a nationally advertised soap powder, rather than simply its cleaning properties. Procter & Gamble started with a low-key approach for its enviro-pak promotion, launching the product in test markets in key cities in 1989, backed up by news releases. This was beefed up at the end of 1990 with a national ad campaign promoting the product's environmental benefits. Marcal U.S. has been selling paper towels, bathroom and facial tissue and paper napkins made of recycled content for years, but now the company is publicizing this green fact in seven-and-a-half-minute videotapes which it sends to retailers for point-of-purchase display. And the American Textile Rental Service Association intends to run an advertising campaign in 1991 to promote the inherent greenness of its member companies product—linen rental services.

The Backlash

The launch of your new green products will undoubtedly attract a great deal of attention. The president of your company or your vice-president of the environment may even become something of a celebrity—Loblaws' David Nichol was quoted in publications around the world when the story of Loblaws' G.R.E.E.N broke. But don't expect all of the attention to be favorable. No matter how carefully you've done your homework, prepared your product and package, researched the issues and green consumer demands, there is almost certainly going to be some kind of criticism. This negative response can come from many quarters: environmental groups, media critics, your customers, your competitors and even the scientific community. Even if you are well prepared they may dent your image, but in most cases you can turn the attendant publicity to your benefit.

Loblaws and Pollution Probe's story is an object lesson in the perils of teaming up with environmental groups whose objectives and ways of dealing with crises are very different from those of the corporate sector. Even the groups that help you develop your green products may do an about-turn after the launch.

Shortly after Loblaws went public with its G.R.E.E.N line the controversy began. Some environmental groups angrily accused Pollution Probe of compromising its reputation by endorsing a line of consumer products. Many environmentalists were especially shocked when Probe's executive director Colin Isaacs appeared in G.R.E.E.N television ads alongside David Nichol, promoting disposable diapers.

"In the best of all worlds," Isaacs told viewers, "everyone would use reusable cloth diapers. But cloth diapers aren't always convenient." Nichol then described why "President's Choice" G.R.E.E.N disposables were environmentally friendly. Isaacs' next move was his most controversial. He urged shoppers, "If you must use disposable diapers, use this one." Disposables had been singled out by some environmentalists as a major contributor to the solid waste problem. These same environmentalists fell over one another to be the first to denounce Isaacs, Pollution Probe and Loblaws, and to cast aspersions on the rest of their green claims. The widely publicized controversy became so ugly—even Pollution Probe started to distance itself from Isaacs, saying he'd acted independently—that Isaacs resigned his position, and Pollution Probe asked Loblaws to stop using its name to promote the line.

The impact of the controversy on Loblaws came in two stages. Initially, press coverage of the G.R.E.E.N line launch was widespread, and cautiously favorable. Manufacturers besieged Loblaws with calls, wanting to know how to produce green products for the line; many delivered prototypes to the company's head office. And consumers responded by purchasing G.R.E.E.N as fast as the company could restock its shelves. After the controversy struck, however, suppliers stopped calling for the most part, and media coverage adopted a critical tone.

An earlier counter-attack had prepared Loblaws for the Pollution Probe controversy (though perhaps not for its ferocity). When the company launched its all-natural fertilizer in the spring of 1989, Greenpeace held a press conference to criticize the product, claiming it contained traces of dioxins and furans. Loblaws had conducted extensive testing of the product, under the watchful eye of Pollution Probe, and the scientific facts themselves disproved Greenpeace's claims. With G.R.E.E.N, the company believed that the public endorsement of an environmental group would add credibility to its products that were already standing on solid environmental footing. "We were surprised and disappointed that our efforts were so roundly dismissed," Patrick recounts. "We believed we were taking important steps by working with an environmental group and developing greener products, and the public pronouncements seemed to us counter-productive."

In the end, the line's extensive media coverage and basic integrity won the day. G.R.E.E.N outsold projections by 50 percent, and is still selling well across Canada and in half a dozen other countries.

Many environmental groups are still accustomed to seeing business as the enemy and deeply distrust current attempts by business to clean up its image. They are ruthless in exposing what they believe to be cosmetic or superficial greening.

It's quite possible that no matter how thoroughly you research your product and how carefully you vet it for hidden environmental flaws, some environmental groups won't be satisfied and will attack you as loudly and as often as they can. However, you're asking for trouble if you don't go the extra mile to make sure that what you introduce into the marketplace is really as green as you say it is.

The counter-attack won't come just from environmentalists either; often consumers and even your own staff may get involved by either boycotting the product, working with the media to reveal the story-behind-the-story or verbally attacking your company in every public forum possible. In the United Kingdom, where green consumerism has been underway for a number of years, consumers are beginning to react against what they perceive as superficial claims by retailers, manufacturers and packagers. They are actively avoiding many green products, in the belief that business shouldn't be rewarded for environmental half-measures. This phenomenon has not yet reached North America, and likely won't become a factor here, because green marketers have already learned from the European experience, and are quickly taking measures to ensure that inaccurate claims and false green products are nipped in the bud.

This doesn't mean a backlash won't happen here; companies are especially at risk if their motives aren't particularly green. The Conservation Law Foundation (CLF) reports that when it was fighting the Department of the Interior over its proposal to loosen restrictions on off-road vehicle use on Cape Cod, Park service staff were among those who felt most strongly that the CLF was right and their employer wrong. Your staff may become the "moles" that supply investigating agencies, such as the EPA, with information needed to act against you, or they may be more high-profile about their opposition, as were loggers who demonstrated against clear-cutting in British Columbia.

The third direction from which the attack may come is your competitors, companies who have decided that greening is too frivolous (or too expensive) and are putting their resources into undermining their competitors efforts to go green. More than one company has launched a green product with much fanfare only to discover that other companies leapt to challenge its validity. These dinosaurs will try to prove that your product is not really green or that it is just as harmful as the product it seeks to replace. In other words, you had better be prepared for criticism from your competitors and be prepared to control the damage when it happens. A quick rebuttal is the best strategy in this case.

A new phenomenon related to the counter-attack from your competitors is the business-to-business boycott, a much more aggressive form of the ripple effect we discussed in Chapter Four. Already several North American companies have chosen to boycott specific suppliers who fail to adhere to their codes of environmental and social responsibility. These corporate boycotters include Apple Computer Company and Ben & Jerry's Homemade. The business-to-business boycott is an example of green corporate activism that brings the initiator excellent publicity while doing great harm to suppliers.

Europe has already seen its first green counter-attack lawsuit. Henkel, a West German chemical manufacturer, launched a phosphate-free detergent, Le Chat, in France, and immediately gained 18 percent of the detergent market. Its largest competition in the market, Rhone-Poulenc, countered with a public campaign that claimed that phosphate-free detergents were more harmful than the standard brands. Henkel sued and won: Rhone-Poulenc withdrew its claim and took down posters of fish supposedly killed by phosphate-free detergent.

This brand of negative reaction is not limited to Europe. In North America, some executives are seeing red over green. The Conservation Law Foundation's staff counsel Armond Cohen says that "there are a lot of utility middle managers who think that conservation is tantamount to communism."

Until corporate greening becomes more complete, the backlash will continue. However, if you are properly prepared, you will be able to weather it with confidence. You can prepare by (1) developing open lines of communication with your critics, or potential critics and by (2) carefully auditing your plans and products for their environmental impact.

By going public with your green products and services, you are still in the minority of North American companies. But the benefits of being early into the marketplace are only going to increase as consumer awareness continues to climb, fresh environmental problems emerge and your competitors scramble to catch up. The green pioneers will play a major role in shaping consumer attitudes and will emerge as North America's most successful companies by the turn of the century.

▫ SEVEN ▫
Green Futures

Throughout this book we have argued that the greening of business is much more than a minor modification of current business practices and standard corporate strategies. It is a fundamental shift in the way we do business. Cleaning up your company and developing environmentally improved products and services requires a shift in your mindset and in every aspect of your operation. As a result of this shift, everyone in your organization, from the CEO to the person on the shop floor, will have to change the way they make decisions. Evidence of this change in thinking is already widespread. It ranges from top executives regularly sitting down with environmentalists to the production of new goods that do not just reduce an environmental problem, but eliminate it entirely.

The key phrase behind this shift is *sustainable development*, which will be central to the new social and economic era we are entering. Visionary green corporate leaders see sustainable development not as a vague, self-contradictory phrase, but as a future economic reality. They believe that economic growth and environmental health are not incompatible; that the planet is not an infinite resource to plunder and pollute, but a precious asset to be managed and maintained. They understand that the days of cheap, abundant raw materials and low-cost energy are all but over. They realize, as Patrick says, "that they can no longer divorce their corporate balance sheets from nature's bottom line." They acknowledge the need to get "more out of less." They may be working as fast as they can to commercialize green innovations and get them to market, but they also see themselves as stewards of the planet with a responsibility for handing a better world over to their children.

These green pioneers are already planning for this future and actively attempting to imagine what it will look like. Although crystal-ball gazing is perilous at best, this chapter is our attempt to identify the most significant near-term trends and to take some educated guesses at the shape of a greener world in the next century as economies move toward the sustainable model. It will provide you and your company with food for thought as you plan for a sustainable future.

Dinosaurs and Dolphins

The changes wrought by the green business revolution have taken place at an astonishingly rapid rate. In fact, the green revolution is proving to be as disruptive as the industrial and technological revolutions that preceded it. If anything, the pace will accelerate as whole sectors experience shakeouts in which the greenest companies leave their competitors far behind. The beginnings of this trend can already be seen in many areas, but a particularly vivid example is to be found in the forestry sector. As we write these words, the North American pulp and paper industry is in the throes of an acrimonious internal debate that is a direct result of the green revolution. The pressures and stakes are enormous. North American pulp and paper revenues exceed CDN$80 billion annually.

The industry's membership is divided over whether to adjust to the new demands or to resist all such changes. Meanwhile, its methods continue to be under attack from environmentalists and growing legions of angry citizens who are outraged by what they regard as destructive forest management and harvesting practices. This rising public concern has encouraged governments to act: as a result over the next three years pulp and paper companies across the continent will have to introduce state-of-the-art pollution-control technology, at a cost of CDN$20 billion dollars. And the pressures are mounting for the industry to change the nature of its product as well. The boom in residential and commercial paper recycling is reducing the market for virgin fiber, while major newspapers—the single largest market for paper—are starting to insist that their newsprint be made from recycled fibre. In 1990, Canada's largest newspaper account, *The Toronto Star*, refused to sign any long-term contracts until it could be assured of a supply of recycled newsprint. In the United States, Gannett and Knight-Ridder are following suit. This is vivid evidence of the kinds of shift in demand that are taking place as a result of the greening of the North American economy.

Pulp and paper companies have responded in various ways to these rapidly changing circumstances. Some have embraced change and are investing in recycling plants, complying with government regulations that call for cleaner processes and advising clients that they can meet their needs for recycled paper. The greenest firms are quietly consulting with environmentalists to develop sustainable forestry strategies, while others are dragging their heels or doing everything in their power to resist the green tide. They argue that their industry isn't the environmental bad guy it is made out to be, point out that plants will close and unemployment increase if uneconomical regulations are enforced. This attitude is so prevalent that the industry's own polls indicate its executives have only a 10 percent credibility rating among the general public.

The pulp and paper industry is only one example of the

phenomenon we call the dinosaurs versus the dolphins. The dinosaurs that once dominated our planet are now extinct because they were unable to adapt quickly enough to massive changes. Dolphins, on the other hand, are among the Earth's most intelligent creatures, and they typify the kind of businesses we believe will dominate the corporate sector in the years to come: fast and alert, sophisticated thinkers and communicators, who consider all aspects of a problem. Our contention is that the more you resist the green business revolution in the short term, the more financially painful it will become. Companies that fail to keep up will go the way of the dinosaur. Industrial museums are filled with products made by companies that were once household words and are now unknown. Around the time the first automobiles appeared, the horse and buggy industry confidently predicted that the number of cars on the roads would be limited to the number of chauffeurs who could be trained to drive them.

Surprisingly, the chemical industry is one sector where dolphin attributes are quickly gaining ground. As a result of a concerted effort to change its practices—reducing emissions at source, for example—we expect this industry to survive in the emerging green marketplace, despite the fact that some chemical companies are continuing to resist change and the industry as a whole remains a favorite target for environmentalists. Although chemical firms still have a long way to go, they were among the first to recognize that public concern was not going to abate and that they had better pay attention to environmental issues. The industry caught the green wave in its early stages and developed much stricter operating standards, threw open its doors to the public, changed its practices and looked for alternatives to its more toxic products. By the early 1990s, a number of companies within the industry were winning awards for environmental excellence.

Over the next decade, the gap between dinosaurs and dolphins will widen. Those who have moved decisively to make their operations, products and services more environmentally benign will increase their profits and their market share at the expense of uncompetitive dinosaurs. This trend may not be as obvious during the current recession; indeed, some corporate executives are using the economic downturn as an excuse to put off green investments. But in the end, this strategy will only leave them further behind. "Environmental issues may fall from the number one spot on the public policy agenda," says environmental consultant Colin Isaacs, "but they won't fall far. Political promises, green marketing, industrial accidents and increased environmental research will ensure the environment remains a high priority with the public." The dolphins profiled in this book are astute enough to know that, while a recession is temporary, the greening of society is not. In fact, they see the recession as a marketing opportunity. The increasing demand for environmental consulting—particularly consulting that cuts packaging and energy costs and improves image—is another sign that greening is here to stay.

Dolphin companies will not only continue to lead, but they will increase their momentum, in part because of the growing ranks of dolphin-type managers. Whether they come into the workforce fresh from a green MBA program or are experienced managers who undergo a green transformation, we believe that this new, green management style will set the pace in the 1990s. Who is this new dolphin? He or she is a natural extension of the new green consumer who expresses a greater concern for social issues and is dedicated to bringing an improved quality of life into the workplace. The dolphin will be conversant with the whole range of environmental issues, their impact on people's lives and their importance in the marketplace. This eco-wise manager will be as comfortable discussing global warming as the stock market and will be adept at spotting emerging green trends locally, nationally and internationally. Dolphin management style will be "sharp but fair"; dolphin managers will take sustainable development into account in making every important business decision.

The Coming Decade

There is no doubt that the changes we have already seen—in public awareness, government regulations, green consumerism and environmental liability to name a few—will widen and deepen. Dolphin companies will do much more than monitor the way these changes affect the evolving green business agenda. They will encourage change by developing allegiances with many of the constituencies that are driving the greening of North American society.

Some business sectors are already involved in establishing the ground rules. However, if your particular business or industrial sector is not already involved in this process, it should be, either through trade associations or established government-and-economy round tables. A number of nations are already moving to develop criteria for sustainable development. The Canadian government recently allocated CDN$25 million to help establish the International Institute for Sustainable Development. The Institute's central objective is to research and report on the links between economic growth and environmental protection. Government leaders, scientists, economists and special interest groups are now establishing the rules of the sustainable development game; your choice is either to watch from the sidelines or participate in the play.

Regulations

Corporations can spend huge amounts of money to defeat proposed legislation—as timber, pesticide, agribusiness and automanufacturers did in 1990, pouring US$35 million into the campaign against California's Big Green—but they are only postponing the inevitable. Regulations will continue to be one of two major forces driving the greening of North America this decade (green consumers will be the other). To wait for regulations to force you to act epitomizes the dinosaur mindset.

To anticipate and plan for the next wave of regulations not only avoids costly disruptions, but also has numerous other advantages—chiefly, a smoother ride with regulators, better relations with the community, lower rates from insurers, a sense of pride or responsibility among employees and an improved chance of attracting investment.

Big Green, in fact, was not defeated by the dinosaur business lobby, but by voters who thought that environmentalists were moving too far too fast. The bill was too complex and tried to include too many sweeping changes in a single piece of legislation. But voters still want to see government put more effort into protecting the environment, and only one in ten North Americans believes that the government is doing a good job of it at the moment. The pressure to introduce new legislation is not likely to abate. Over the short term at least, most people in government and industry agree there will be an increasing emphasis on new regulations.

What will the regulatory picture of the 1990s look like? We predict that there will be many more regulations than there are today, and standards will rise as science develops and refines its ability to measure environmental damage. Literally thousands of regulations are now on the drawing board in the United States and Canada. Internationally, the trend is on a par with North America. Most important, there is likely to be a transferring of power from the federal level to states, provinces and local municipalities. Community activism has resulted in the merging of two trends: a growing demand that environmental regulations be enforced and a growing desire to design legislation at the local level, so that control and enforcement remain in community hands.

Although some states have panicked and are rescinding tough environmental laws, the overall trend is to introduce laws ahead of federal regulations. Vermont Governor Madeleine M. Kunin, a proponent of progressive legislation, notes that "states can lead by example." In 1990 Kunin issued an executive order to reduce energy use in Vermont by 20 percent and greenhouse gas emissions by 15 percent by the year 2000. Other regions are enacting similarly tough and independent measures, and voters are expected to resist any attempt to take this new-found power out of their hands. This is another fundamental reason why business must move to support overall standards at federal and international levels. That way the patchwork of often conflicting legislation enacted by local communities won't determine how businesses operate and where they can market their products, and hamper their ability to make national and international sales. The other end of the regulatory spectrum will see governments begin to encourage sustainable practices through the use of green tax incentives.

A recent government initiative in The Netherlands shows the probable shape of things to come. The Netherlands' National Environmental Policy Plan (NEPP), developed in consultation with business, community groups, environmentalists and other special interest groups, aims to clean up The Netherlands in a single generation. It will accomplish this through (1) integrated product-life-cycle management that closes resource loops to reduce emissions and waste; (2) increased energy efficiency; and (3) improvements in the quality of all products to reduce toxins and prolong the usefulness of resources. NEPP may forbid disposables and planned obsolescence altogether.

This sweeping program relies on voluntary compliance for many of its provisions, including the elimination of asbestos in automobile brake linings and an ongoing commitment to refillable containers (versus disposable) from both beer and soft drink manufacturers. The plan's rationale is to fix the environmental problem at the intake pipe, rather than at the outlet, reasoning that the current band-aid approach to pollution abatement consumes ever-increasing amounts of the GNP, and rarely solves the basic problem. The costs of this new scheme will be offset in part by energy savings and reductions in the cost of raw materials, but Dutch industry will still have to pay approximately 88 percent more for environmental measures in 1994 than they did in 1988, the agricultural sector will see a 179 percent increase in costs, and households 138 percent hike.

Whatever form legislation takes, it will continue to be a major factor in shaping the way business is managed in the coming decade, and well into the twenty-first century. Companies can wait to be legislated into action or they can recognize the inevitability of greening and work with governments and other stakeholders to develop regulations that meet everyone's objectives. Government-mandated eco-labeling, developed in reaction to the increasing demands of green consumers, is another example of how legislation will affect your operations in the years to come, even if it is not yet a factor for your country, company or industry. Environmentally progressive countries already have detailed plans in place to help consumers decide which products are best for the environment and why. These are being discussed in North America, so it makes sense to become involved now in establishing eco-labeling standards.

Greener Citizens

Whether voting at the ballot box or the cash register, there is no avoiding the powerful impact of green citizen action. Politicians aren't setting the green agenda, their constituencies are, and the corporate sector knows it is no coincidence that this green revolution is referred to as "market-driven." We believe that community-based environmental activism will be the force to be reckoned with this decade. For example, early in 1991 when this book went to press, despite the fact that North America was in the throes of a recession and in spite of public resistance to tax hikes, citizens were telling pollsters that they nonetheless supported a green tax. In 1990, according to *U.S. News and World Report*, 69 percent of Americans said they would be willing to approve a tax hike to pay for pollution control or environmental improvements. In Canada in the same year, 73 percent of the populace stated their willingness to pay a green tax, according to Environmental Research Group Ltd.

There are other indications that awareness and activism will increase. Canada's new Environmental Protection Act includes provisions that will soon allow ordinary citizens to take environmental matters into their own hands, for example, to sue landlords who refuse to make their buildings healthy. In the European Community, there is talk of an "environmental bill of rights" that would allow citizens to take polluters to court. In the United States where class action suits are firmly entrenched in law, such environmental activism will likely have a major impact.

The phenomena we are witnessing in the early 1990s is described by Patrick as Higher Inner-Consciousness Consumers (HICCs). "These people make decisions based on ethical, moral and environmental concerns," he says, "and these consumers are going to use their shopping carts to push for a better world." They have become increasingly demanding and selective: they will reject excess packaging, will insist on information about a product's and package's content and will insist on knowing if a product's manufacture, use or disposal will be harmful to their families or the environment. HICCs are signaling both their concern for the environment and their willingness to change their habits to help improve it.

We believe that after the initial wave of green consumerism has subsided a more significant trend is likely to develop. First there will be a broadening of green product and service lines so that there will almost always be a green alternative. By the turn of the century there will begin to be a marked reduction in per capita consumption. As the emerging values of the HICC become more entrenched and raw materials increase in price, North America will move away from being a throwaway society where built-in obsolescence is the norm to being what has often been called a conserver society, characterized by goods that cost more but last much longer. "In the near future, when you see a road side sign that reads 'garage sale'," Patrick notes, "it will mean that the garage is for sale. Our accepted practice of buying inferior quality and disposing of it in this way will disappear."

As the social pendulum swings away from the concerns of the "me generation" and consumers become more focused on the collective good of their decisions, there will be a resurgence of interest in cooperatives. Already, the cooperative movement numbers more than 600 million members worldwide; and cooperatives today don't just offer farmers a way to manage their grain—there are manufacturing and construction co-ops as well. Surprisingly, Japan has one of the fastest growing memberships with 16 million members at the end of 1990. Perhaps cooperatives will be the multinationals' main competitors in the next century.

The already environmentally aware citizens will be further galvanized by the bad news that will emerge over the next few years. Irrefutable evidence of the impact of global warming will emerge soon, our sources say, and indications are that it is much worse than expected. Ozone depletion will get much worse before it gets better, causing more and more people to contract skin cancer or develop cataracts. Horrifying stories of environmental abuses behind the Iron Curtain will emerge as Eastern Bloc countries open their borders to Western investment.

What does all of this mean for business in the short-term? Each of the areas we have covered in this book—strategic planning, product development, packaging, corporate image-making—will have to be constantly revised. CEOs will have to become more comfortable with environmental issues and deal regularly with activist organizations. In the 1990s, senior executives will clearly be spending more time meeting with these former foes and working out ways of cooperating with them. Environmental education is ensuring that the generation coming out of school this decade is highly sensitized to the planet's environmental crisis. This new generation will include many aggressive proponents of sustainable development.

Business and Environmental Organizations

In the coming decade alliances between business and environmental groups will increase in number as corporate and environmental mindsets merge. Meanwhile, it will become ever more difficult to distinguish mainstream environmentalists from businesspeople. Already, companies are not only inviting environmentalists into their organizations to act as consultants, to join their boards and to help educate their staff, but businesspeople are venturing even further into green camps. By the end of 1990, the boards of some major environmental organizations, such as the National Wildlife Federation, included representatives from corporate senior management, in some instances presidents and CEOs.

However, the road ahead has quite a few potential potholes. Just as there is disagreement about strategy within the pulp and paper industry, environmental organizations will experience a similar split amongst their members. The less moderate environmentalists will continue to attack the more moderate organizations, accusing them of selling out to the enemy. This will lead to a growing division between environmental groups as the mainstream struggles to distance itself from the radical fringe. The mainstream groups will become more sophisticated in their business knowledge, and in their technical and financial ability.

What will the new environmental group strategies be in the 1990s? A likely target will be the major multinationals who have so far avoided the greening process or shifted questionable operations to less strict jurisdictions. At the same time these groups will try to build on and expand their current business alliances. The McDonald's Environmental Defense Fund task force that is underway as this book goes to press indicates the possible scope of these undertakings. This task force will review all aspects of McDonald's operations that contribute to waste generation—the supply and distribution systems as well as the operation of individual restaurants and it will explore ways to reduce, reuse, recycle and compost the waste. Importantly, the contractual agreement between the two is very specific about each organization's intention and obligations. Each side has a variety of escape hatches. McDonald's insists that it be able to interpret the recommendations of the task force as it chooses and to quit at any time if things aren't working out. EDF refuses to allow McDonald's to use its name in any advertising, and if the company abandons the recommendations of the report, the EDF is free to publicize and advocate its own conclusions from the results of the study. "We believe," says EDF executive director Frederic D. Krupp, "that the project will create a blueprint for the entire fast food industry." The success or failure of the task force will play a major role in determining the kind of working relationships we can expect to see between business and environmental groups in the future.

New Opportunities/New Industries

The fresh thinking that typifies the work of the green pioneers who are factoring the environment into their everyday thinking will become commonplace in the 1990s. Leadership will come from the business sector as ideas like using waste as a new source of raw materials and market-incentive legislation become accepted norms. All existing sectors will experience a shift in their markets due to increasing costs at both ends (raw materials and disposal) and the growing demand for environmentally benign products and services. "There is no doubt that environmental issues will have priority in the 1990s," says David Weinberg, President of CIBC Development Corporation (the development arm of the Canadian Imperial Bank of Commerce). "Our challenge will be to identify the associated private and social costs."

In Chapter Two we identified some of the new business opportunities that are already emerging. The rest can only be guessed at, but there are two basic types of opportunities that we can see developing: (1) new applications for existing technology, products and services and (2) new products and entirely new industries.

One example of changing perceptions can be found in the case of Power Screen, an international resource-sector equipment company. One line of Power Screen's equipment—machinery for extracting mineral resources—has been modified to solve the growing garbage crisis. In a test site in Collier County, Florida, this machine is now "mining" landfill. Disposed materials are dug up and sorted into four piles: scrap such as tires and large appliances that can be sold; ferrous metal that can be sold; an organic mixture that can be composted or used to cover the landfill each day; the remaining plastic, wood and rubber can be recycled or burned in an incinerator to generate power. The result of this new application of an existing piece of technology is thousands of dollars of savings for the local municipality and a huge potential new market for Power Screen.

The demand for greener operations and the increasing expense and difficulty of disposing of waste will intensify. Already industry demands for improved environmental management have created a major corporate sector, the environmental protection industry. This sector includes companies that conduct environmental assessments and audits, monitor your operational emission levels and test your products and waste for their environment-friendliness. It also comprises consultants who help you plan your green corporate strategy and train your staff in new green procedures and waste management firms, energy management companies and firms that manufacture pollution-control technology and equipment. In North America alone, the environmental protection industry is worth in the neighborhood of US$16 billion annually and has grown by 32 percent since 1983. It is expected to grow an additional 13 to 18 percent this decade.

The British and Germans currently lead the world in the development of this sector, but excellent opportunities still exist for North American firms in this expanding market. In particular, waste management firms such as Laidlaw Environmental Services and chemical giants such as Du Pont have already recognized the new business potential. For example, waste management firms are active in developing municipal recycling programs, and chemical firms are busy setting up parallel businesses to clean up toxic wastes. (A number of chemical firms have developed their own environmental clean-up programs, in the process discovering that they could offset their research and development costs, and even turn a profit, by marketing their expertise to other companies.)

New concepts and designs in transporation, urban development and communications will dominate the marketplace of the 1990s. The following are three areas that we expect will be key sectors as the ecological business perspective becomes more dominant:

1. *Biotechnology.* Certainly the most powerful and probably the most controversial of the new industries, "biotechnology" is the term coined to describe a broad area that includes the manipulation of molecules, genes, bacteria and other building blocks of life. The new applications for these altered elements include environmental control (such as the clean-up of oil spills), health care (for instance, in developing the cure for life-threatening diseases), resource maximization (for example, breaking down wood pulp to extend its usefulness) and agriculture (so that food can be produced year round, eliminating any down time of equipment, land or livestock).

2. *Ecotourism.* As developing countries begin to realize that they can make more money in the short-term and protect their natural resources over the long-term by opening their doors to sightseers, efforts will be made to develop or strengthen tourism. There is already a growing market among green consumers for travel to "untouched" regions.

3. *Energy.* The motto for this sector will be: "An energy dollar saved is a dollar on the bottom line." This idea will become more popular as the decade progresses—both because energy costs will rapidly escalate, and because resource maximization will become mandatory for companies who want to remain competitive. There will be more shifts in regulatory requirements that will allow utilities to make a profit by selling efficiency. Although North America used about US$150

billion less energy in 1990 than in 1989, it still uses two times as much energy per dollar of GNP as do Japan and some European countries. Alternative energy sources will also come of age as more companies explore ways of producing their own power. Although Germany is currently the largest manufacturer of solar panels in the world, many interesting experiments utilizing both solar and wind power are taking place in North America today.

In short, as happened in the industrial and technological revolutions fortunes will be made by the companies that move first to meet the new demands of the new marketplace. Imagine the rewards for the business that develops the perfect transportation device: a vehicle that is made from recyclable and lightweight parts, that uses the earth's natural magnetic field for power and that runs as quietly as a bicycle. Such a vehicle is no harder to visualize today than a NASA space shuttle would have been at the time of the Wright brothers. But given the human capacity for innovation many of the solutions to environmental problems will be developed by the very sector that is now generally pointed to as the culprit: industry. The green revolution will ensure new opportunites for the companies that move fastest, and that keep an eye on the horizon. These pioneers embrace environmental problems as opportunities awaiting solutions.

The Twenty-First Century

By the turn of the century the move toward sustainable development will have clearly manifested itself in the way the North American and world economies operate. Accompanying this move and playing a central role in its progress will be the rise of geonomics, the new economic system we discussed in the opening chapter. Geonomic theory says that continued growth can only be achieved by making environmental costs an integral part of doing business. The early stages of geonomics are already here: stricter standards for emission control, more expensive liability insurance, escalating landfill costs, environmental audits and environmental-impact assessments are all part of the cost of doing business in the 1990s.

As we become more knowledgeable about the economic impact of business on the natural environment, new costs will be added to the ledger. The range of questions companies and countries face as they come to terms with this entirely new economic system is daunting. What are the full costs of industrial activities? What is the real value of a non-renewable resource? How do we debit our national accounts for the use of raw materials? Because such issues are international in scope and because they cover territory that is totally new and involve the concerns of countless different interest groups, we believe that developing a working geonomic model will be one of the most complex and difficult tasks facing society in the next century.

An important tenet of geonomics is that as we begin to pay for the "services" provided to us by the earth's natural assets— everything from the land and the atmosphere, to the seas—our use of these resources will become much more sparing. One of the geonomist's first priorities will be to attribute a value to all natural resources.

As we begin to take these "new" costs into account our traditional economic indicators will have to undergo dramatic change—either being modified to include such costs or replaced by entirely new sytems. The GNP, for example, records the impact of an environmental catastrophe in a different way today than it would under geonomics. An industrial accident now shows up as a net benefit: the demand for medical personnel and clean-up crews for a chemical leak, oil spill or nuclear accident generates considerable economic activity, which means that the GNP rises. Under geonomics the loss of natural resources and the environmental damage resulting from such an incident would mean a decrease in the GNP. In the words of Robert Repetto, senior economist of the World Resources Institute, a green think tank based in Washington, D.C., "under the old system a nation could exhaust its natural resources, cut down its forests, erode its soils, pollute its acquifers, hunt its wildlife to extinction, with illusory gains in income and permanent losses in wealth."

The current Gross National Product measures the total value of goods and services generated in a country each year. The new, green GNP would include calculations for *natural* capital, as well as *humanly-created* capital—everything from fossil fuels and minerals to wetlands and farmlands. Geonomists argue that the human economy is only a sub-system of the overall biosphere. Because it does not exist in isolation, any calculations that ignore the natural world are inaccurate. The development of this new system will ultimately be international in scope. One of the first steps toward the development of a green GNP will be to conduct "environmental audits" of entire countries so that a complete inventory of the world's natural resources can be established— including both "fixed" stock (such as land) and "renewable" stock (such as forests).

The introduction of geonomics will be paralleled by a growing demand for scarce resources, everything from fossil fuels to land. This increasing demand will ultimately lead to increasing costs for business, which in turn will be passed on to consumers. We believe that the end result of this economic revolution will be a social revolution, where everyone begins to use resources more frugally and efficiently. A gradual move away from consumption and toward conservation will take place, largely because there will be no choice.

Consider one of the key factors that is contributing to this major shift in perspective. Apart from declining resource stocks and escalating costs, the world's major environmental problem today is explosive population growth. In the 1950s, the planet's population was 2.5 billion; by 1986 it had doubled. The increase in human beings since 1940 is equal to the population growth since the first humans appeared on this planet. By 2025, the United Nations predicts, there will be 8.5 billion people on earth. Ninety-five percent of these people will be in underdeveloped countries, and will be, in economic terminology, "acting to maximize their own interests." As the *Brundtland Report* pointed out, the Third World's growing middle class has no intention of going without the consumer goods that the rest of the world currently takes for granted.

This will lead to two developments. First, as geonomics emerges there will be a growing realization on the part of these nations that their natural resources are worth more than the value placed on them today by international markets. Secondly, since environmental pollution knows no borders, underdeveloped nations will recognize that their contribution to cleaner practices is crucially important; as they begin to industrialize they will demand the help of the developed world in introducing the best available technology. There is no doubt that under geonomics industrial countries will be required to stop exploiting the resources of peripheral nations. When Japan imports trees from Indonesia it will not simply pay for the raw logs, but also for Indonesia's resource depletion, ensuing environmental pollution, dislocation of indigenous people and associated health costs.

What other impact will the greening of the economy have on the marketplace of the twenty-first century? One commodity that we take for granted today will become much more valuable than oil or silicon chips—food. Nations that act now to ensure that they are world leaders in sustainable agriculture will, in our estimation, be well-positioned to lead the new world economy. The population figures cited earlier combined with the scarcity and declining quality of arable land will create a shortage of this most precious resource. Today, farmers are an endangered species, but with a renewed emphasis on agriculture they will resume their central economic role. In fact, we predict that self-sufficiency in food will become an integral part of every nation's national security plan. Concurrent with the emergence of agricultural self-sufficiency, and despite a world-wide trend toward global trade, we expect to see a countervailing move toward more autonomous trading. This will develop as countries take stock of their resources and discover that these are not as bountiful as once believed. As a result, nation states will begin to live within their own ecological means. It is impossible to predict how this situation will evolve, but ultimately we expect to see global trade largely limited to controlled quantities of essential resources.

Gradually, green thinking will become more fully integrated into the North American way of life and into our business practices. This will result in new government policies, institutional changes and altered decision-making practices. The corporate field of vision will broaden beyond merely meeting the needs of consumers to include the concerns of the entire community. Sustainable development will be challenging to implement and the manner of its implementation will vary between countries and industries, at least in the short-term. The question is not can we achieve this new economic order, but do we have the will to. The green pioneer's answer is yes.

The twenty-first century holds great promise for dolphin companies who are preparing today for a more sustainable future. We can only begin to imagine what the Fortune 500 will look like in the year 2000, but it will be very different from today. The green marketplace of the twenty-first century will be based on a conserver society where all costs—social, environmental and economic—are included in the cost of doing business, and where green will always be more valuable than gold.

▫ Appendix One ▫
A Green Business Library

The following are books we recommend as useful additions to every company's green business library. Many of them were seminal in the development of *Green Is Gold*.

Agriculture

The Cornucopia Project. *Empty Breadbasket: The Coming Challenge to America's Food Supply and What You Can Do About It*. Emmaus, PA: Rodale Press, 1981.

Canada, The Standing Committee on Agriculture, Fisheries and Forestry to the Senate of Canada. *Soil at Risk: Canada's Eroding Future. A Report on Soil Conservation*. 1984. Ottawa: Senate of Canada

Wilford, Allen. *Farm Gate Defense: The Story of the Canadian Farmers' Survival Association*. Toronto: N.C. Press Ltd., 1985.

Economics

Block, Walter E. *Economics and the Environment: A Reconciliation*. Vancouver: The Fraser Institute, 1989.

Daly, Herman E. and Cobb, John B., Jr. *For the Common Good: Redirecting the Economy Toward Community, the Environment and a Sustainable Future*. Boston: Beacon Press, 1989. This book begins where conventional economics leaves off; an excellent introduction to ideas that may help solve our environmental predicament.

Doern, G. Bruce. *The Environmental Imperative: Market Approaches to the Greening of Canada*. Toronto: C.D. Howe Institute, 1990.

Mungall and Mclaren for the Royal Society of Canada. *Creating Alternative Futures: The End of Economics*. New York: Oxford University Press, 1978.

Schumacher, E.F. *Small is Beautiful: A Study of Economics as if People Mattered*. London: Abacus Edition, 1974. A groundbreaking theory of economics.

Environmental

Berger, John J. *Restoring the Earth: How Americans Are Working to Renew Our Damaged Environment*. New York: Anchor Press, 1979.

Carson, Rachel. *Silent Spring*. Boston: Houghton Mifflin Company, 1962. This book is frequently singled out as one of the first to bring international attention to environmental problems, particularly the bioaccumulation of pesticides.

May, Elizabeth. *Paradise Won: The Struggle for South Moresby*. Toronto: McClelland and Stewart, 1990. This book is an excellent overview of current debates over forest management, and the lengths to which different interest groups are willing to go to oppose major logging companies.

Thompson, William Irwin, ed. *G.A.I.A.: A Way of Knowing, Political Implications of the New Biology*. Great Barrington, MA: Inner Traditions, Lindisfarne Press, 1987.

Van Den Bosch, Robert. *The Pesticide Conspiracy*. Berkeley, CA and Los Angeles, CA: University of California Press, 1978.

Environmental Auditing

Greeno, J. Ladd et al. *Environmental Auditing: Fundamentals and Techniques,* rev ed. Cambridge, MA.: Arthur D. Little, 1985. From the pioneer in the field, environmental auditing from A to Z, written so that novices can easily understand the process.

Richmond, John, ed. *Industrial Waste Audit and Reduction Manual: A Practical Guide to Conducting an In-Plant Survey for Waste Reduction*. Toronto: Ontario Waste Management Corporation, 1990.

The Future

Rifkin, Jeremy with Ted Howard. *Entropy: Into the Greenhouse World,* rev. ed. Toronto: Bantam New Age Books, 1989. Some powerfully held views of the adverse consequences of moving too quickly into a brave new world. Rifkin is particularly critical of the biotechnology industry.

Weiner, Jonathan. *The Next One Hundred Years.* Toronto: Bantam, 1990.

Zuboff, Shoshana. *In the Age of the Smart Machine: The Future of Work and Power.* New York: Basic Books, 1988.

Green Consumer

Elkington, John and Julia Hailes. *The Green Consumer Guide: From Shampoo to Champagne, High-Street Shopping for a Better Environment.* London: Gollancz, 1988. The first book of its kind, this one paved the way for all other editions of "how to shop green" books.

Pollution Probe et al. *The Green Consumer Guide.* Toronto: McClelland and Stewart, 1989. Based on the book by Elkington and Hailes, and published with the support of Loblaws, this book was a major Canadian best-seller.

Politics

MacNeill, Jim, Fen Osler Hampson, Nonita T. Yap and Rodney R. White. *International Journal: The Greening of World Politics.* Toronto: Canadian Institute for International Affairs, Volume XLV #1 Winter 1989-90.

Porritt, Jonathan. *Seeing Green: The Politics of Ecology Explained.* New York: Blackwell, 1984.

Spretnak, Charlene and Fritjof Capra. *Green Politics: The Global Promise.* rev. ed. Santa Fe, NM: Bear and Company, 1986.

Reference

The National Wildlife Federation. *Conservation Directory.* Washington, 1991. An annual listing of environmental organizations across North America (national, state/provincial and local), as well as government agencies concerned with the environment.

Eiserer, Leonard A.C., ed. *World Environment Directory: Standard Environmental Reference.* Silver Spring, MD: Business Publishers, Inc. 1990. A listing of individuals and companies that are involved in environmental activities in North America.

Sustainable Development and Geonomics

Hammond, Dr. Allen L., ed. *World Resources: A Guide to the Global Environment.* New York: Oxford University Press, 1990.

Hirschhorn, Joel S. and Kirsten U. Oldenburg. *Prosperity without Pollution: The Prevention Strategy for Industry and Consumers.* New York: Van Nostrand Reinhold, 1990.

Starke, Linda. *Signs of Hope: Working towards Our Common Future.* New York: Oxford University Press, 1990. An international survey of the progress countries, organizations and businesses have made in implementing the recommendations of the Brundtland Commission.

Troyer, Warner. *Preserving Our World: A Consumer Guide to the Brundtland Report.* Toronto: Firefly Books, 1990. An easy-to-read overview of the major recommendations of the Brundtland Commission.

The World Commission on Environment and Development. *Our Common Future.* New York: Oxford University Press, 1987. The report of the Brundtland Commission; includes an examinations of the critical environmental and economic issues our society faces, and suggestions for dealing with these problems.

Worldwatch Institute, *State of the World: Progress toward a Sustainable Future*. New York: Norton, 1990.

□ Appendix Two □
The Environmental Experts

The following national and international organizations have a stated interest in working with the corporate community.

North American

(These organizations are in operation in both the United States and Canada and often in other countries.)

Canada-United States Environmental Council
United States: James G. Deane, Defenders of Wildlife, 1244 19th Street NW, Washington, D.C. 20036   (202) 659-9510
Canada: Paul Griss, Canadian Nature Federation, 75 Albert Street, Ottawa K1P 6G1   (613) 238-6154
Works to enhance the exchange of information on environmental issues between the two countries.

Ducks Unlimited, Inc.
United States: One Waterfowl Way, Long Grove, IL 60047
(708) 438-4300
Canada: 1190 Waverly Street, Winnipeg, Manitoba R3T 2E2
(204) 477-1760
Mandate is to develop, enhance and preserve waterfowl and other wildlife habitats; assists other organizations in accomplishing similar goals.

Friends of the Earth
United States: 218 D Street, SE, Washington, D.C. 20003
(202) 544-2600
Canada: 251 Laurier Street West, Suite 701, Ottawa, Ontario
K1P 5J6   (613) 230-3352
Through lobbying and public education works to reduce toxic chemicals in the environment, protect the ozone layer and to highlight the dangers of certain pesticides; affiliations in thirty-six countries.

Greenpeace
United States: 1432 U Street NW, Washington, D.C. 20009
(202) 462-1177
Canada: 578 Bloor Street West, Toronto, Ontario M6G 1K1
(416) 538-6470
This group of activists on the political left works to protect the environment; specific concerns include whaling, nuclear and hazardous wastes.

Sierra Club
United States: 730 Polk Street, San Francisco, CA 94109
(415) 776-2211
Canada: 2316 Queen Street East, Toronto, Ontario M4E 1G8
(416) 698-8446
Focusing on forestry issues and preservation of wilderness areas, the Sierra Club describes itself as middle-of-the-road, but also activist.

World Wildlife Fund (in Europe, known as *World Wide Fund for Nature.*)
United States: 1250 24th Street NW, Washington, D.C. 20037 (202) 293-4800
Canada: 60 St. Clair Avenue East, Suite 201, Toronto, Ontario M4T 1N5   (416) 923-8173
The international organization's goal is to protect wildlife and habitat; senior corporate executives of host countries play an active role; no membership—donations only, to support specific projects.

U.S.-based

(Some of these organizations operate in other countries as well.)

Audubon Society
950 Third Avenue, New York, New York 10022
(212) 546-9100
Conservation objectives include the management of 250,000 acres of wildlife sanctuaries; 500,000 members.

Center for Environmental Information
99 Court Street, Rochester, New York 14604 (716) 546-3796
Provides education and information services for government, industry, public interest groups.

Climate Institute
316 Pennsylvania Avenue, SE, Washington, D.C. 20036
(202) 547-0104
Conducts research on global warming for public policy makers.

The Conservation Foundation
1250 24th Street NW, Washington, D.C. 20037 (202) 293-4800
Affiliated with World Wildlife Fund United States; research, education and technical assistance on land use, risk assessment and environmental dispute resolution.

The Conservation Fund
1800 North Kent Street, Suite 1120, Arlington, VA 22209
(703) 525-6300
Advances land use and water conservation ideas in partnership
with other organizations, including business.

Conservation Law Foundation
3 Joy Street, Boston, MA 02108-1497   (617) 742-2540
Works to improve environmental protection, resource management and conservation. Has achieved notable success in developing energy-efficiency programs with United States utility
companies.

Council on Economic Priorities
30 Irving Place, New York, 10003   (212) 420-1133
Publishes *Shopping for a Better World*, an annual booklet that
rates companies according to their ethical and environmental
practices; presents an annual environmental achievement award
to corporations.

Cultural Survival, Inc.
11 Divinity Avenue, Cambridge, MA 02138 (617) 495-2562
Works to protect the rights of indigenous peoples; alliances with
business include importing of goods from the world's rainforests;
has programs on five continents.

Environmental Defense Fund
257 Park Avenue South, New York, 10010   (212) 505-2100
Respected research organization; combines scientific, economic
and legal disciplines to develop sustainable solutions; joint task
force with McDonald's Corperation; idea for tradable pollution
credits included in new United States Clean Air Act.

National Resources Defense Council
40 W 20th Street, New York, New York 10011 (212) 727-2700
Develops strategies to protect the environment through legal
action, research and public education; worked successfully to
develop energy-efficiency programs with utilities.

National Wildlife Federation
1412—16th Street NW, Washington, D.C. 20036 (202) 637-3700
Works to preserve wildlife; respected in political circles for its
effective environmental lobbying; claims 4 million-plus
supporters.

The Nature Conservancy
1815 N Lynn Street, Arlington, VA 22209 (703) 841-5300
Key objective is to preserve plants, animals by purchasing lands
these organisms need to survive; accomplishes this objective by
working with a number of organizations, including business.

Rails to Trails Conservancy
1400 16th Street, NW, Washington, D.C. 20036 (202) 797-5400
Works with organizations to develop greenspaces in urban areas,
chiefly along abandoned railway lines.

Resources for the Future
1616 P Street NW, Washington, D.C. 20036 (202) 328-5000
Research and education on conservation and efficient use of
natural resources; social-scientific and economic in focus.

Rocky Mountain Institute
1739 Snowmass Creek Road, Snowmass, CO 81654-9199
(303) 927-3851
A green think tank concerned chiefly with promoting energy
efficiency, but also with alternative energy sources. Believes that
energy conservation is more vital than military spending to
national security.

Wildlife Habitat Enhancement Council
1010 Wayne Avenue, Suite 1240, Silver Spring, MD 20910
(301) 588-8994
Encourages corporations to enhance their undeveloped lands for
the benefit of wildlife, fish and plant life.

The Windstar Foundation
2317 Snowmass Creek Road, Snowmass, CO 81654
(303) 927-4777
Encourages individual responsibility for development of sustainable future, chiefly through education.

World Environment Center, Inc.
419 Park Avenue, Suite 1404, New York, NY 10016
(212) 683-4700
Serves as a bridge between industry and government, in an effort
to strengthen environmental management and industrial safety.

World Resources Institute
1709 New York Avenue NW, Washington, D.C. 20006
(202) 638-6300
Helps governments and the private sector work toward natural
resource management, economic growth and other long-term
environmental goals; publishes *World Resources Report*, an annual
analysis of the issues related to environment and sustainable
development.

Worldwatch Institute
1776 Massachusetts Avenue NW, Washington, D.C. (202) 452-1999
Well-respected green think tank that studies and reports on global
environmental issues; publishes influential annual *State of the World*.

Zero Population Growth
1400 16th Street NW, Washington, D.C. 20036
(202) 332-2200

Objective is to achieve a sustainable balance between population, resources and development; active internationally.

Canada-based

(some of these organizations are based in other countries as well.)

Canadian Arctic Resources Committee, Inc.
One Nicholas Street, Suite 412, Ottawa, Ontario K1N 7B7
(613) 236-7379
Education and information exchange on environmental, social and economic issues of northern development.

Canadian Coalition on Acid Rain
112 St. Clair Avenue W, Suite 401, Toronto, Ontario M4V 2Y3
(416) 968-2134
Works with business and special interest groups to reduce sulfur and nitrogen-oxide emissions into North American atmosphere.

Canadian Environmental Law Association
517 College Street, Suite 401, Toronto, Ontario M6G 4A2
(416) 960-2284
Uses current environmental laws to protect environment; works to develop better environmental legislation in Canada.

Canadian Environmental Network
P.O. Box 1289, Station B, Ottawa, Ontario K1P 5R3
(613) 563-2078
Information-sharing network of more than 1200 environmental groups across the country; publishes an updated reference list on these organizations each year.

Canadian Nature Foundation
453 Sussex Drive, Ottawa, Ontario K1N 6Z4 (613) 238-6154

Its stated goals are evironmental education and preservation of endangered species and habitats.

Canadian Wildlife Federation

1673 Carling Avenue, Ottawa, Ontario K2A 3Z1
(613) 725-2191
Information and education to foster understanding of natural environment.

Energy Probe

355 Lesmill Road, Don Mills, Ontario M3B 2W8 (416) 444-8419
Respected green think tank on energy-related issues, conservation and renewable resources.

Harmony Foundation of Canada

P. O. Box 4016, Station C, Ottawa, Ontario K1Y 4P2
(613) 230-7353
Promotes education and information on environmental issues; emphasis on developing programs with corporate sector.

The Nature Conservatory of Canada

794A Broadview Avenue, Toronto, Ontario M4K 2P7
(416) 469-1701
A sister organization to the United States group, its primary objective is to acquire and preserve "ecologically significant" land areas in Canada; works with select organizations to achieve this goal.

Pollution Probe

12 Madison Avenue, Toronto, Ontario M5R 2S1
(416) 926-1907
Active in issues involving toxic wastes, water quality, solid wastes and the environment and foreign policy; works with business, government and the public to educate and inform.

□ INDEX □